Helion & Company Limited
Unit 8 Amherst Business Centre
Budbrooke Road
Warwick
CV34 5WE
England
Tel. 01926 499 619
Email: info@helion.co.uk
Website: www.helion.co.uk
Twitter: @helionbooks
Visit our blog http://blog.helion.co.uk/

Published by Helion & Company 2021
Designed and typeset by Farr out Publications, Wokingham, Berkshire
Cover designed by Paul Hewitt, Battlefield Design (www.battlefield-design.co.uk)

ISBN 978-1-914059-19-3

British Library Cataloguing-in-Publication Data
A catalogue record for this book is available from the British Library

We always welcome receiving book proposals from prospective authors.

CONTENTS

Abbreviations 2
Foreword 2
Preface 2
Acknowledgements 3

1 Culture and the Argentine Navy 4
2 Culture, Strategy and the Falklands/Malvinas Conflict 18
3 Culture and Operations in the South Atlantic 33
4 Conclusion 67

Bibliography 72
Notes 76
About the Author 80

Dedication

To my parents, Silvia and Jorge

ABBREVIATIONS

ARA	Armada de la República Argentina (Argentine Navy)
ASW	anti-submarine warfare
ATP	Allied Tactical Procedure
CIC	Combat Information Centre
CO	commanding officer
COAN	Comando de la Aviación Naval Argentina (Argentine Naval Aviation)
ELMA	Empresas Lineas Maritimas Argentinas (Empresas Argentinas Sea Line)
ESOA	Naval Officers School (Argentine Navy)
HMS	Her Majesty's Ship
HQ	Headquarters
JAP	Permanent Advisory Board (Argentine Navy)
NATO	North Atlantic Treaty Organisation
SATO	South Atlantic Territory of Operations (Argentine Navy)
SS	steam ship/screw steamer
RRS	Royal Research Ship
TF	Task Force
UK	United Kingdom
UN	United Nations
UNASUR	Unión de Naciones Suramericanas (Union of South American Nations)

FOREWORD

As the son of an officer of the Argentine Naval Academy's class of 1945, it is an honour for me to write the foreword to this important work by Jorge Bóveda, who investigates the causes and consequences of a recent and painful chapter of our naval history. On the other hand, as a political scientist who has studied the impact of cultural variables on political and operational outcomes, I have found it particularly interesting to immerse myself in this research that contributes to the understanding of a serious national frustration.

Bóveda´s analysis is sensitive to successes and failures of the key admirals of our navy. He spares no substantive criticism and never falls into the temptation of easy praise. Looking ahead, his observations generate knowledge that enables an important transfer from the academic sector to the military sector.

The spirit that guides the work is related to that of the Athenian Thucydides, who created scientific historiography by removing mythology from the study of history. Athens lost its Peloponnesian war just as Argentina lost its Falklands/Malvinas War. Similarly, in their stories, Thucydides and Bóveda draw strength from weaknesses, without allowing the reveries of false patriotisms to sterilise the fecundity of their analysis.

Bóveda claims for Argentina the recovery of a full national state status. With good reason, he suggests that if by failing to make the investments needed to keep ourselves strong, we abdicate from our defence, we will become something less than a state, informally subordinated to more orderly and sensible neighbours who did not commit our self-destructive errors.

This is not just a scientific work. It is also a work committed to our Republic and its destiny. As an intellectual born in the great Argentine naval family, I am honoured and delighted to participate in its presentation in society.

Carlos Escudé
Ph.D. (Yale '81) Senior Research Fellow (Retired) at CONICET

PREFACE

In a sense the roots of this book can be traced back to my childhood. Indeed, I was just 11 years old when I came to the United Kingdom for the first time, sometime in June 1972. My father was then a recently promoted Lieutenant Commander and an electronic engineer – graduated with honours at ITBA University in Buenos Aires – and had been sent there for six months – which soon extended to three years – to take several technical courses related to the electronic equipment of the most modern warship of the Argentine Navy, the brand new Type 42 guided missile destroyer ARA *Hercules* – sister ship of HMS *Sheffield* – which at that time was still in the early stages of construction at Vickers' shipyard in Barrow-in-Furness, in the northwest of England. Little did we know that 10 years later they would be fighting each other under different flags.

My father quickly embraced the British way of life, so much so that he even started pipe smoking, like many of his Royal Navy colleagues. Like the majority of Argentine naval officers, he felt privileged to work side by side with one of the world's major naval powers and member of NATO. He was invited to all relevant social events of the Royal Navy, and Argentina received the treatment given to an important and strategic client. He learned to admire and respect the British folk, and when he finally left in 1975 had a distinct anglophile flavour around him, like many others who had followed the same path.

The Falklands/Malvinas War has been subject of numerous research papers that have focused mostly on tactical issues and only superficially address the motivational aspects and performance of the service as a whole. During my research undertaken in 2014 for my Master´s degree in Strategic Studies I came across Alastair Finlan´s brilliant book on institutional culture and strategy – focused on the Royal Navy – that immediately seized my attention, as no such equivalent existed for the Argentine Navy.

My lifelong interaction with naval officers and dozens of interviews with war veterans – for a previous book – plus my access to the then-classified official documents of the Argentine Navy in the South Atlantic War gave me all the key elements to put together a thesis proposal in order to provide a much-needed cultural interpretation of the Argentine Navy and its relation to modern combat that will contribute to open new lines of research in areas still unexplored by historians, while at the same time allowing valuable conclusions to be drawn for the future.

By January 1980, I had joined the Naval Academy as an officer cadet at the age of 18 – today some of my classmates have reached the rank of rear admirals – and, although I only stayed for a year, I experienced the process by which civilians are turned into naval officers. Later as a lawyer and adviser to the ex-Navy Centre for Strategic Studies and as a permanent member of the Editorial Board of the Naval War College Review, I had the opportunity to work closely with senior naval officers and came to appreciate the immense influence of institutional culture throughout the service. Remarkably, this phenomenon is hardly recognised within the Argentine Navy and, in general, is subconscious in nature to those serving within the institution, even though it accounts for much of the rationale and reasoning of the Navy itself.

Chapter 1 offers an analysis of how culture is produced, replicated and sustained within the officer corps of the Argentine Navy as well as its relationship with the concept of strategic culture. Chapter 2 addresses the strategic predilections of the Argentine Navy. It also examines the unprecedented challenge and operational requirements that the Navy had to overcome during the Falklands/Malvinas War to confront the British Task Force, no other than the third naval power in the world, that had from the outset the assistance and logistical support of the US Navy. An assessment of the Argentine Navy around 1980 and the problems that had begun to manifest towards the end of the decade is also included. Chapter 3 develops the impact of institutional culture on naval operations, with particular emphasis on the lack of inter-service coordination during the war. The Chilean factor is briefly examined given the fact that it had a great influence on the Grand Strategy adopted by Argentina during the conflict. Finally, chapter 4 outlines a conclusion from the perspective of institutional culture, in addition to illuminating future scenarios for the Argentine Navy in the 21st century.

The aim of this book is to illustrate a rarely considered aspect of the Argentine Navy and how it influences not only the day-to-day life of the service, but also major decisions during time of war. My conclusion is that institutional culture can account for much of the successful performance in combat of the Argentine Navy, despite being a naval service that had to grow and develop without the test of combat, due to the long periods of peace that the country's history went through.

It also attempts to show that the Argentine Navy of 1982 had a very qualified and highly professional officer corps. These remarkable men turned second-hand equipment into a first-class combat system capable of causing millions of pounds worth of damage to the enemy. They also developed an aggressive strategy – executed by the Etendard/Exocet system – that kept both British ASW aircraft carriers at bay, and managed to hit a third deck – Atlantic Conveyor – which at the time was on station in the heart of the British Battle Group. The big freighter was full of helicopters and other essential war materials. All this was done with a very limited supply of Exocet missiles. Finally, their expert weapons engineers were able to create from scratch a state-of-the-art land-based Exocet battery that did not exist in the world market, which was able to hit the destroyer HMS *Glamorgan* putting her out of action for the rest of the war.

Thus, the very modest Argentine Navy made its mark during the South Atlantic conflict at tactical and strategic operational levels. As this book will show, little has changed since the 19th century in terms of institutional culture, except of course for the hardware and the speed of modern naval warfare: the people were just the same, the spirit in the ships was just the same, and the courage of the men was just the same. If the Argentine Navy´s institutional culture remains intact, despite the huge juncture that currently faces, then the results will continue to reflect the best of Argentina´s naval traditions.

Last but not least, it is important to note that the analysis, conclusions and views in this book are completely my own and should not be associated with the Argentine Ministry of Defence or the Argentine Navy.

ACKNOWLEDGEMENTS

This book is based on my Master's thesis, which in common with research of any nature has many patrons. First and foremost, I am very grateful for the patience, counsel and support of my supervisor, Dr Jorge R. Bergallo, Head of the Postgraduate Studies at the Argentine Naval War College, National Defence University. I have also been very fortunate in the number of people who have helped directly or indirectly with the production of the thesis. The Archive of the Argentine Navy provided me with considerable assistance and I am very appreciative of the advice from former Director Captain (retired) Enrique Isola who made available all relevant material in regard to the Argentine Navy official navy records. Special mention is due as well to Captain Argentine Navy (retired) Gabriel Catolino, for his illuminating thoughts about the navy culture. I am also in debt to my friend Rear Admiral Marcelo C. Tarapow, for his technical advice on several matters.

In the course of examining various aspects of the Falklands/Malvinas conflict I managed to interview many key personalities involved in the campaign and I am grateful to the following for their hospitality as well as frank opinions: the late Admiral (retired) Jorge Isaac Anaya, Vice Admiral (retired) Juan José Lombardo,

Vice Admiral (retired) Benito Rótolo, Rear Admiral (retired) Carlos Büsser, Rear Admiral (retired) Julio Marcelo Pérez, among many others. From the diplomatic service I interviewed Dr Carlos Ortiz de Rozas, former ambassador to the UK in 1982; the late Dr Oscar Camilión, former Foreign Minister of General Viola in 1981; Dr Juan Carlos Beltramino, former Argentine ambassador to the UN in 1982. Readers will note that I have omitted any references to these interviews, with the sole exception of Ortiz de Rozas, as much of the information contains personal views on the Falklands/Malvinas Conflict that I consider inappropriate to reveal in such a public forum.

Special thanks are due to Professor Alastair Finlan – Swedish Defence University – for his kind advice and support and, in a way, for having inspired this book. I am also indebted to my friend and colleague Dr Mariano Sciaroni for his unflagging support to this project.

Finally, my warmest thanks to Dr Carlos Escudé for his generous preface to this book.

1
CULTURE AND THE ARGENTINE NAVY

Argentina has to the east an extent of 4,725 km of maritime coast, a huge jurisdictional sea with its continental shelf, plus the archipelagos and islands that make up the heritage under her control: all these elements confirm that the Argentine Republic is by nature a maritime nation. However, only a very small part of the population has chosen to serve in the navy and enter this unique brotherhood.

Since the birth of the Argentine Navy some 200 years ago the naval profession has distinguished a certain type of individual that requires special capabilities and a distinctive mindset that offers some insight into how and why naval officers think differently from others. That explains in part why even today, in the advanced missile age and in spite of so many sophisticated weapons systems at hand, the human element has remained the most important factor in warfare.

These individuals represent a minority occupation in Argentina and are the practitioners of naval warfare in the Southern Cone, normally on a smaller scale than the rest of the world. They have joined a profession in which the fundamental purpose is to apply force – sometimes lethal – to attain military, and ultimately, political ends. The key contribution of the Argentine Navy to the country´s security is the conduct of operations *at* and *from* the sea. Neither analogues nor substitutes exist. These professionals, unlike in most other occupations, may never practise their skills after an average career span of 30 years. Their performance in war – a haphazard event – ultimately depends on Argentina´s foreign policy, which managed to get them out of harm's way for 120 years, until the Falklands/Malvinas War. It was during this 74-day conflict that a window opened to observe the Navy´s strategic culture for the first time in a war environment. Regardless of this totally unexpected event, the naval profession continues – even during extended times of peace – to attract people all over the country, despite the fact that the occurrence of war in Latin America is at present practically inexistent.

A-4Qs in close formation sometime in 1980. (Argentine Navy)

German built MEKO 360 (Almirante Brown-class) destroyers which entered in service in the post-Falklands/Malvinas War period. (Argentine Navy)

Military Organisations

The armed forces are centuries-old institutions that represent one of the most important organisations within a state. These organisations provide the foundational element on which the political structure resides. They are designed with a specific purpose; in the particular case of the Argentine Navy, to provide a force option within the maritime environment, in order to secure the nation's maritime interests.

The Argentine Navy is a very old military institution, which has existed for about two centuries. As such it has served the country in various ways not only at war but also as a link to far away Argentine dominions like Patagonia, which were literally isolated without the intervention of the navy. Although very modest in naval platforms, if compared to the navies of the major powers, it has nothing to envy with regard to discipline and work spirit. Since the country´s independence, the Argentine Navy has always had an active role in the defence of national sovereignty, in support of our foreign policy, and an outstanding performance in search and rescue missions, which have earned her the recognition of countless nations operating in Antarctica. Let us review very briefly some of these interventions:

In November 1903 the corvette *Uruguay* under the command of First Lieutenant Julian Irizar – later Vice Admiral – achieved the successful rescue on the white continent of the Swedish scientific expedition led by Dr Otto Nordenskjold, placing the Argentine Navy – without knowing it – for the first time in the international headlines.

Years later, during the Spanish Civil War (1936-1939) the Argentine Navy had a new opportunity to serve the country, this time by giving shelter to Spanish citizens who had requested the right of asylum in the Argentine legation in Spain to escape from certain death in the war. By an executive order from President Agustin P. Justo and with the approval of Congress, the cruiser ARA *25 de Mayo* – under the command of Captain Miguel Ferreyra – was sent first, and later relieved by the destroyer ARA *Tucumán* – under Commander Mario Casari – saving thousands of men, women and children refugees from sure death at the hands of the Republicans, many of whom never returned to the motherland.[1]

Argentina was also the first country to support the blockade and quarantine against Cuba, which President Kennedy declared on the occasion of having discovered in October 1962 the installation of military bases for Soviet intercontinental ballistic missiles in that country. On 28 October Argentina sent two destroyers, ARA *Espora* (D 21) and ARA *Rosales* (D-22), to operate with a multinational Task Force under the command of Rear Admiral (USN) John A. Tyree. Despite the vertiginous development of events, the quick response of Latin America – and Argentina in particular – demonstrated immediate and decisive support for US policy in what was perhaps one of the closest moments to a nuclear confrontation that the world has ever lived. The Latin American support was decisive for the diplomatic battle that Washington waged against Moscow. It was perhaps the last major episode of the Cold War.

In 1982, during the South Atlantic conflict, the Argentine Navy´s Fleet Air Arm displayed great courage and professionalism above and beyond the call of duty by sinking one guided missile destroyer of the British Type 42 (HMS *Sheffield*, D-80), a Type 21 frigate (HMS *Ardent*, F-184), and an important logistic ship (SS *Atlantic Conveyor*) of the enemy Task Force with just 12 fighter jets, using new naval aviation tactics: the air-to-surface Exocet AM39 missile, thus becoming a pioneer of these new techniques, never before used by any country.[2]

In September 1990, the Navy intervened in Operation Desert Shield – now as an ally of the British – in the First Persian Gulf War (1990–1991) by sending Task Force 88 under the command of Captain Eduardo A. Rosenthal (later Rear Admiral, retired).[3] In this way the Argentine Navy was part of the coalition of countries that defeated the Iraq of Saddam Hussein.

A decade later the Navy once again hit the world headlines of the local and international press in the summer of 2000 with the successful rescue by the icebreaker ARA *Almirante Irizar* (Commander Eugenio Fachin) of the passenger ship MS *Clipper Adventurer*, which had been trapped in the ice pack near the Antarctic Peninsula.[4]

Early Days of the Argentine Navy

The man who first understood the importance of a regular navy for Argentina was Captain Clodomiro Urtubey (1840–1902), who had graduated with honours as a midshipman in 1865 from the San Fernando Naval Academy in Spain, an institute where he had been sent by the government. It was this distinguished officer who proposed to President Sarmiento's Minister of War, Martin de Gainza – by memorandum of 12 July 1871 – the creation of a small-scale naval academy aboard the ship under his command. The proposal became Law 568 and was approved by executive order on 5 October 1872. The so-called Nautical School was installed in the steamer *General Brown*, Urtubey being appointed as her first commandant.[5]

Sarmiento was no stranger to the advantages of having a regular navy, something he had witnessed during his stay in the United States shortly after the end of the American Civil War. It was there that he made contact with some Confederate naval officers who would later provide invaluable services to the country. During that period, he also became familiar with the new weapon systems of the US Navy, where a new type of ship – the monitor – and the introduction of a new weapon – the electric torpedo (contact mine) – stood out as a new underwater device of great destructive power, which could be operated manually from the coast.[6]

After Sarmiento was sworn in as president, the Argentine Congress approved the first law of naval armaments in May 1872, which allowed the construction in the United Kingdom of the first Argentine fleet to provide some sort of defence to the city of Buenos Aires and at the same time control the access to the River Plate estuary. That modest brown-water fleet went down in history as *Sarmiento´s Squadron*, from which the old gunboat *Uruguay* – later reclassified as corvette – with mixed-propulsion (steam and sails) still remains afloat in downtown Puerto Madero. Acquisitions of naval platforms and dock facilities on land to provide support to the fleet were strategically oriented to the defence of the River Plate and, in particular, the city of Buenos Aires.[7]

Since the independence of the nation, a defensive way in warfare prevailed for the country´s naval forces, which legitimately sought to consolidate what the land armies achieved with their continental campaigns.

But it was President Julio A. Roca, two times president of the Argentine Republic (1880–1886 and 1898-1904) and former Minister of War, who argued, a decade before Alfred Mahan, that 'the [Argentine] State should rely firmly on the sea, in order to ensure the prosperity of its trade, and project abroad, in order to sustain the role of the Republic in American and world politics'.[8]

Argentine Navy Style of Warfare

The strategic military planning of the current Argentine Republic also establishes an eminently defensive style of warfare for our armed forces, which favours cooperation – with other states – but at the same time allows the country to implement any defensive measures to protect the state, adapting it to the regional and international context and to the ethical principle that aspires to avoid war to settle disputes.[9]

Within this framework, naval operations must be carried out following the nation´s vital interests, which are marked by the political authorities, taking into account the particularities of the aquatic environment, especially around its complex interaction with other states and the international legal system that governs it.

Admiral Segundo Storni pointed the way forward by warning national authorities that 'naval policy is, above all, a government borne initiative; but it is indispensable, in order to have nerve and continuity, that its objectives take root in the entire nation, that they are a clear idea, a conviction of the ruling classes, and a constant aspiration of the entire Argentine people'.[10]

The search for peaceful settlements to resolve conflicts does not contradict the need to have naval forces at readiness for a battle at sea. The translation at the tactical level of the primary mission of the Argentine Navy remains the naval battle, and the central activity of

The century-old Sailing Ship *President Sarmiento* as seen in Puerto Madero today. (Argentine Navy)

our naval military instrument is precisely the preparation to deal with that contingency.

However, without ignoring the advances in the relationship between the armed forces and society, in general the obstacle of collective ignorance on the subject persists, although at different levels and even in several countries worldwide. At present, this symptom is no longer an isolated event; it is also linked from a more general perspective, with the progressive political apathy shown by current societies on issues of the state in general and on defence matters – characteristically in peacetime – in particular and everything that concerns the armed forces.

This explains, in part, the absence in Argentina of state policies regarding defence issues since the advent of democracy in 1983 to date. According to Carlos Escudé, 'it is an involution that begins with the Falklands/Malvinas War, deepens with the military dimension of the neoliberal policies of the 1990s, was aggravated by the emerging budget straits of the 2001-2002 crisis, and culminates with the government´s punishment to the military corporation from 2003 onwards'.[11] At the moment, there are no regional complicated scenarios in the Southern Cone, but if there were, we do not know if our armed forces are in a position to fulfil their mission, because there is still an absent debate: the role of the armed forces in Argentina;[12] something that it is incomprehensible in a decade where our neighbours are rearming constantly, and in which different regional forums such as the Union of South American Nations (UNASUR) have been created to achieve common objectives in this area with the friendly countries of the region.

Creating a Military Culture

Military organisations, due to their exclusive nature, tend to be relatively isolated from the environment as a standard mechanism of self-reproduction of their own inner workings. In the case of the armed forces, this tendency towards secrecy is more pronounced by its special function of the use of force that obliges them to hide information about their resources and their operations.[13] In modern democracies – with professional, all volunteer armed forces – only a select few are chosen to join the ranks of the military. In the Argentine Republic, for example, approximately 18,555 people (trained) serve in the contemporary Argentine Navy,[14] in the absence of a mandatory military service, which means that only a very small fraction of the 45 million inhabitants of the country experience close contact with the naval service.

In spite of this deliberate secrecy, the Argentine armed forces have continued to prepare for war. Access or a lack of it has not altered their primary purpose that is none other than 'conjure or repel any external military aggression that puts our sovereignty and territorial integrity, and the life and property of our inhabitants at risk'[15] or – as Bernard Brodie once said – 'to win wars'.[16] This is the inner core around which military culture is formed. In the field of international relations, a large part of contemporary research begins to focus on the role of culture within these organisations.

Culture is an abstraction, however the forces that are created in social and organisational situations that derive from culture are very powerful. If we do not understand how these inner forces operate, we will become victims of them. In order to understand an organisation, it is necessary to analyse both the visible and the most subtle and invisible factors, that is, their characteristic cultural elements.

The culture of a military organisation is commonly associated with the set of values, norms, beliefs, doctrine and formal and informal knowledge that shapes the collective understanding. According to Ralph Kilmann, 'culture is to the organisation, what the personality is to the individual, it is what provides meaning, direction and mobilisation'.[17] The institutional culture acts as a sort of normative and social amalgam that holds the organisation together and expresses the values and ideals that members of an organisation share. As a consequence of sharing the same cultural identity, a social order, a collective identity and a collective commitment of one over another are created that crystallises in what we could call the *esprit de corps* that unites and characterises the different states of the armed forces.

Multiple cultures may exist within a single social entity – for example community, organisation, state and so forth – but there is always a dominant one that is interested in preserving the status

Aircraft carrier ARA *25 de Mayo*, flagship of the Argentine fleet, sailing somewhere in the South Atlantic during 1980. (Argentine Navy)

quo. Hence, culture can be an instrument of control, consciously cultivated and manipulated.[18]

The critical question is that of how a military culture can be evaluated or measured. Military establishments create a methodological challenge for researchers seeking to explore the visible and invisible aspects of the service. In that context we understand that a study that addresses the relationship between institutional culture and modern warfare, with specific reference to the Falklands/Malvinas War of 1982 and its connection with strategic culture, is a breath of fresh air in the extensive bibliography of the conflict.

To that end, we will adopt a qualitative and sociological analysis based on interviews with war veterans who played leading roles during the South Atlantic conflict, the official documents related to the Falklands/Malvinas War held by the Argentine Navy,[19] the very few memoirs that have been published from the Argentine side, and other public and private documents. Additionally, we will illustrate how culture is formed and perpetuated among the officer corps of the Argentine Navy in the initial stages, based on first-hand observations.[20]

The focus on the officer corps is deliberate, because it provides the leaders who make the key decisions within the organisation. As Legro observes, 'Cultures, once established, tend to persist. Those individual members of a culture who adhere to its creed tend to advance in an organisation and become the dominant culture´s new protectors.'[21] It is through people, or more specifically officers, that military culture is replicated in a uniform manner over extended periods of time.

The Argentine Navy

The Naval Academy at Rio Santiago is the place where the cultural regeneration process occurs for the newly joined officers. It is an initial training establishment that introduces the new cadets in the beliefs, norms and values of the naval service for four years before determining whether or not they are fit to integrate the officer corps.

Once the first four very demanding years of studies at the Naval Academy have been left behind, the cadets carry out the final tests during a round the world trip on board the sailing ship ARA *Libertad* during the fifth year, if successful they graduate with the rank of midshipmen. For months they sail the seas of the world, practicing the acquired knowledge and performing on board the functions inherent to the officer corps. They practice seamanship, navigation and all related issues of the naval profession, for which the Naval Academy has trained them, consolidating in this way the *esprit de corps* that must characterise the men and woman of the service. At the heart of the organisation are the basic assumptions and beliefs, which are taken for granted and that are invisible.

Explaining the way in which the Argentine Navy generates a cultural format requires a multi-disciplinary approach. We will have a closer look at the process of converting a civilian to a military officer.

Making a Naval Officer

Alastair Finlan argues that 'Military leaders are artificial creations, shaped and manipulated by institutions to conform to their own image.'[22] In the Argentine Navy the new officer cadets must go through a very hard selection and training process that could be described as intense indoctrination. The civilian or potential officer is immediately displaced from mainstream Argentine society in a physical and psychological sense by being immersed in an all-encompassing military environment. Quite quickly in this setting, the former civilian begins to transform himself into a military officer, which is particularly noticeable among new recruits after just four weeks of intense training. An individual´s entire life structure is completely altered to fit in the service. The process of assimilation stretches from personal appearance, such as haircut, dress and bearing, to attitudes and beliefs. The Argentine Navy achieves this goal in its training process in a remarkably short space of time. This occurs during the so-called recruitment, which lasts, as already said, 30 days. In that period the cadets are confined to the establishment and work for periods that average 16 hours a day. During that time, they develop all sort of activities (academic, sports, navigation, sailing, etc.). Gradually through instruction, hard training and the military environment the recruit becomes navalised. Dropouts, and those considered unfit for naval life, are quickly excluded from the main group.

Each cadet is assigned a *tutor* – a 4th year cadet – who acts as an adviser or guide, that is, someone to turn to if there is a problem or situation that merits the advice or intervention of a senior cadet. This tutor can be very useful during the first year at the Naval Academy, which is when the greatest dropouts occur.

Identity within individual divisions and classes is promoted on a daily basis. Competition with other recruits and other units is inculcated from day one and it remains an essential element of a naval officer´s career. If at any stage a naval officer or a cadet leaves the service, the bonds are so strong, that normally they continue to be in close contact with the Navy and their former comrades. However, within the institution the bonds are broken and that person is replaced immediately by others: a brutal selection process that has honed generations of naval officers in the jungle of advancement to higher ranks. By the time a naval officer reaches the rank of full admiral – four stars – of the service, that of Chief of the General Staff of the Navy, then the institution will have selected an individual who reflects the beliefs and assumptions of the service to a greater degree than his contemporaries.

The social separation from society is most effectively achieved through the use of institutionally specific language. The language of the Argentine Navy revolves around the terminology associated with ships. Lots of technical terms are rapidly assimilated, for example, *Bravo Zulu* means *well done*, and so on.

The sustenance of this navy mode within the Argentine Navy is heavily dependent on people. Culture is always constructed, maintained and reproduced by people. It is people that create meanings and understandings. In the Argentine Navy, people are very important in acting as role models for new recruits. Behaviour and values are rigorously sustained by strong codes of discipline clearly set out in writing in the Naval Regulations, a number of publications that cover virtually all aspects of conduct for officers and ratings in every possible scenario, from which uniform to wear on a particular day to disciplinary codes for inappropriate behaviour. In this sense, naval society is governed by explicit codes, which have been in existence within the institution for centuries. As Finlan rightly sustains, 'Uniformity and conformity are the twin bedrocks of behaviour.'[23] Individualism that falls outside of the group is simply not tolerated. Underpinning the social codes of the Argentine Navy is the importance of *fitting in*, which is derived from ship-borne existence in which an individual who does not fit in disrupts operations on board ship, what can be highly hazardous whether in peace time or at war.[24]

The closed society of the Argentine Navy creates an institutional reality, which permeates everything. As Finlan points out: 'Everything is provided for within naval life, from a regular income, accommodation and food to social events. From this perspective, institutional culture is not only all pervasive but also generates a high level of dependency among its personnel.'[25] The Argentine Naval family is literally *one for all and all for one.*

Protected Cruiser *General Belgrano*, one of four ships of Italian origin which were the core of the Argentine fleet at the beginning of the 20th century. (Argentine Navy)

Argentine dreadnought ARA *Moreno* (30,500 tons) entered service in 1915 with her sister ship ARA *Rivadavia*. At the time, these were the most powerful warships in Latin America. (Argentine Navy)

The DNA of the Argentine Navy

Military doctrines are the equivalent of what sociologists call *meanings*, that is, a determined and typified conventional response to deal with a previously defined situation (a threat, an incoming attack, an emergency, etc.). They express, simultaneously, training, education, history and culture. Knowledge of the sources of a given doctrine of an armed service is one of the best ways to understand it and to predict its behaviour in the face of a given situation.

The White Book of Defence defines doctrine as 'the organic body of essential concepts, principles, criteria and rules that guide the preparation and use of the military instrument, both in times of peace and war; and what they do to fulfil their mission'. [26] In other words, the so-called doctrine represents what is taught in military establishments about war and the art of fighting.

Argentine naval history teaches us about the bold incursions of privateers that spanned the South Atlantic and the Pacific Ocean, reaching up to California, Hawaii and the Philippine Islands. But Argentine regular naval forces in their genesis were confined to brown-water theatres. During the war of independence against the Spanish Navy, the theatre of operations was the River Plate. The same situation arose during the war against the Empire of Brazil (1826-1827). In 1838-1848 the fight was against the Franco-British joint forces on the Paraná River. The confinement to such a restricted environment was imposed by regional political events and the country's poor resources, although Argentina was defending itself against a foreign aggression.

The Triple Alliance War (1869-1872) declared by Argentina, Brazil and Uruguay pursued rejecting the invasion undertaken by Paraguay to Mato Grosso (Brazil) and the Province of Corrientes (Argentina). The war arena was the upper Paraná River, where the Argentine Navy was only able to play a secondary role, falling on Brazil the direction of naval operations.[27]

The evolution to a blue-water navy aroused as a response to a precise stimulus: the need to ensure sovereignty over Patagonia. Given the rapid Argentine economic development, in the period 1860-1890, which made Argentina one of the 10 richest countries in the world, the high seas fleet became a tangible reality. But a true strategic thought had not yet been shaped, despite the modernisation and expansion of the Navy after the near clash with Chile at the end of the last century.

Admiral Segundo R. Storni – graduated at the top of his class of the Naval Academy – was the man who initiated the development of strategic thought in the Argentine Navy. Storni was a leading specialist in international law – known and respected outside the country – and at the same time a brilliant officer, prophetic geopolitical adviser and leading strategist. In 1916, with the rank of commander, he gave two lectures at the leading newspaper *La Prensa* that laid the foundations of a doctrine he called *Argentine Sea Interests*, which in a short time became the basic maritime policy of the country.

When he delivered his lecture, Storni was a follower of Mahan. Later, he had access to the works of the French naval theorist Raoul Castex, eventually synthesising the works of both naval thinkers. In 1930, already a captain, he was assigned the mission of presiding over a commission whose objective was the reorganisation of the Navy.

The Storni committee exerted a great influence on the development of naval doctrine. A master plan was established and

Stern view of the dreadnought ARA *Rivadavia*. (Argentine Navy)

The battleship ARA *Moreno* after her modernisation in US shipyards in 1926. (Argentine Navy)

applied during the term of Admiral Eleazar Videla as Naval Minister, in which many senior officers were trained and indoctrinated. One of the paramount points of the plan was the foundation of the Naval War College, based on the French strategic orientation and the North American operational concept. 'Since then,' – says Rear Admiral Fernando A. Milia – 'Argentine strategic thinking has essentially been a "champagne and bourbon" cocktail.'[28]

The officers, following that doctrine, were trained in what was then called general tactics. They studied procedures, instructions and rules on how to manoeuvre at sea before and during a naval battle. The influence of the *ATP1* (*Allied Tactical Procedure*) began then, but the adhesion to the North American tactics began even before, at the beginning of 1920s, and was applied firstly to naval aviation and then to the submarine force. Subsequently, the Marine Corps and the surface fleet adopted the North American tactical doctrine.[29]

In the whirlwind of an agitated national context, the Argentine Navy had to endure a process that involved two major changes of national identity: the Hispanic and the strong Italian migratory currents. The surprising thing is that the Navy retained its Hispanic roots and style. But it was, and continues to be, open to all sources of doctrinal or technological influence, or to any experience that could contribute to its warfighting improvement. Despite Hispanic roots, staff training continues to respond to a French pattern, like many other aspects of Argentine culture.

As for the operational doctrine, its origin comes from French and North American sources, which were melted forming a national doctrine, by way of articulation of how the navy prefers to fight. However, doctrine is not specific in relation to place, opponent and time. For the CO the doctrine is essentially context-free. By adding the context, the applicable doctrine is transformed into tactics, operational art and strategy. The CO acts as the creative force, aware of the guidelines of the doctrine, but adapting it so that it fits into the specific context of the assigned mission. In this way the tactic, not the doctrine, solves the question: How should I use the naval forces in combat against the adversary X in the place Y at the time Z with the weapons, organisation and information I have?

In short, the Argentine Navy is the final product of a unique historical and sociological process, which began with the emergence of Argentina as an independent nation and whose contemporary period encompasses a century of peace. This long and peaceful process was a blessing for the country – and a challenge for the navy – which had to develop, without the test of combat.

William Brown: Cultural Touchstone

One of the most powerful symbols within the Argentine Navy is that of William Brown. The selection of Admiral Brown to represent the *ideal image* of the naval officer, from a broad spectrum of former

The captain, officers and ship's company of the first crew of the ARA *Rivadavia* in 1915. (Argentine Navy)

and distinguished naval officers, is indicative of his personal and professional prestige within the institution.

Brown – although Irish by birth – embraced the cause of the United Provinces of the River Plate (now the Argentine Republic) during the War of Independence, in which he had a distinguished performance. He was a skilled commander who had served in the American and British merchant navies, where he obtained rapid promotions, thanks to his undeniable conditions as a leader and his ascendancy over his subordinates. His tactical genius and strategic vision allowed him to obtain resounding victories in the River Plate estuary, which earned him recognition in Argentina as the father of the Navy.

Possibly the most important and remembered of the naval campaigns in which he participated was that of 17 May 1814, when – with a poorly armed squadron – he ended Spanish rule in the River Plate, facing a much stronger Spanish foe. The very next day the city of Montevideo fell, leaving General José de San Martin free to start his liberating campaign. This naval victory, due to the magnitude of its strategic effects, is annually commemorated as Argentina´s Navy Day.

Brown spent much of his life at sea, although in these latitudes we remember him for his naval victories in the River Plate. The naval war (in the river and maritime arena) provided the stage where its naval career flourished and consolidated. Therefore, the Brownian image is constructed on the foundation that warfare is the most desirable vehicle toward success in the Argentine Navy. In personal terms, his gender and morals are very significant. Apart from his masculine nature, Brown was a family man, a fervent Catholic and a very much respected figure in social aristocratic circles.

As a gifted leader, Brown was a man who maintained a very close bond with his subordinate commanders. Gender and its social portrayal are also an important issue in the Argentine Navy. All of the naval commanders who have distinguished themselves in combat to this day, are men (Brown, Bouchard, Espora, Rosales, Molini, Gomez Roca, Rótolo, Bedacarraz, Mayora, Curilovic and so many others). A cult of masculinity, which inevitably includes male bonding, does exist within the Argentine Navy, which is perfectly natural in an organisation with a hundred percent of its history generated and maintained by men.[30]

The bonds of camaraderie are explicitly reinforced by the Brownian image, particularly by the notion of *band of brothers*, where success in combat is the result of men who work jointly, side by side as a team, underpinning the so-called *esprit de corps*.

The Argentine Navy actively encourages officers from the beginning of their careers not only to work together, but also to spend as much time together as possible in all sorts of activities: sports, parties, etc. Consequently, the levels of interaction are much more intimate than in most other professions, more akin to family than workmates, and all personal and professional life are known to all. Brown represents a cultural touchstone for the Argentine Navy and the preservation of the old historic surface ships, for example the sailing-training ship *President Sarmiento* and the century-old corvette *Uruguay*, both afloat in Madero Harbour – Puerto Madero – an exclusive neighbourhood in downtown Buenos Aires, being both a symbol of success and status to the contemporary Argentine Navy. It is well known that the Chief of Staff of the Navy – head of the Argentine Navy – still uses the sober and refined day cabin of the frigate´s captain, which is not open to the public, for important service meetings. The symbolism is self-evident.

Sustaining a Military Culture

Military organisations usually divorce themselves from their surrounding society as a means of maintaining levels of identity. The environment of the Argentine Navy is dominated – as in many other navies – by the image of the surface ship or the warship, which represents more than the historical means through which the Navy has obtained its greatest glories. It is a symbol in itself within the institution. Therefore, surface line officers are considered the cream of the crop of naval service and are the ones who generally reach the rank of four-star admiral and are in charge of the service. The other branches of the Navy, such as submariners, marines and aviators rarely reach that rank within the service.

At the beginning of the 20th century the tour of duty of an officer aboard a warship was duplicated in terms of years of service; today that criteria no longer apply in the Navy, but the years of service embarked – as head of department, second in command or captain – are always seen by the service as prestigious positions, and constitute an important step in an officer's career towards higher rank and more demanding posts.

Captain Felix Dufourq on board the training ship *President Sarmiento* with HRH the Zar Nicolas II of Russia. (Argentine Navy Photo)

When the line officers reach the rank of lieutenant commander in the second or third year, they must attend the Naval War College in order to aspire to command a warship of the surface fleet. This special training is also mandatory for the officers of the professional branch – doctors, lawyers and engineers – as a previous step for promotion to higher rank and more senior posts.

Already in the first decades of the century, the Argentine Navy considered the US Navy as a role model in terms of doctrine and methodology in naval operations. Therefore, when the Naval War College was created in 1934, it started out with American advisers. This explains why for many years its staff included three to six US Navy officers. Subsequently, under the umbrella of the military aid program, this group of advisers was transformed into a US naval mission, but initially they were advisers selected by the same Argentine Navy, who paid them for their services. The consequence of this was that the Navy had a selected group of advisers to train its officers, who later had an outstanding performance in the US Navy.

The American influence is completed with the almost annual training of Argentine officers in the Superior Course of Command and Strategy in Newport, Rhode Island, USA, experience that is compensated by sending some officers to other war schools in other countries – for example France, Great Britain, Chile and Brazil. The graduates from the US Naval War College are known within the force as the *Newport boys* and– with the sole exception of one case – all have reached flag rank.

After completing the Naval War College, graduates may be eligible to carry out their first command. Ship commands, in the career of an officer, are divided into three categories: for a lieutenant commander (3rd class command), for commanders (2nd class command) and for captains (1st class command).

Norms are the other element that represent one of the most important aspects of the institutional culture of the Argentine Navy. These norms, along with the customs and habits allow to anticipate the behaviour pattern and attitudes of serving personnel. These invisible rules allow to reach the values that are implicit in them.

The importance of norms does not lie only in their compliance. Compliance becomes enforceable because it allows to achieve certain ends or values that are often not clearly perceived – that is, non-quantifiable, non-measurable abstractions – but that possess the power of ethical or moral imperative difficult to avoid. However, they fill our lives and guide our individual actions and facilitate our understanding and social behaviour in order to live in peaceful harmony.[31] The high level of consistency between officers in terms of behaviour can only be accounted for by the universal adoption of norms.

Values and Subcultures

In the Argentine Navy values represent the core of institutional culture within the service and is the trade mark that distinguishes the Navy from other organisations. According to Professor Mary Jo Hatch, values are 'the social principles, goals and standards held within a culture to have intrinsic worth'.[32] These golden values can be divided into two categories: professional and personal. On a professional level, the primary value universally recognised by the service is that the state needs its Navy to defend its sovereignty at sea and her maritime interests along its extensive maritime coastline, a task that cannot be delegated to any other service. War, conflict or any use of force has enormous legitimacy within the Navy in order to perpetuate its existence. Underpinning this value is a loyalty to the country, the flag and the elected political authorities, who will decide how and when the service will be deployed.

Professional values among naval officers – regardless the subculture they serve: surface officers, naval aviators, marines or submariners – are quite homogeneous given that all are graduates of the Naval Academy, generating a marked cohesion between the cadres and an indelible *esprit de corps*, one that subsists even years after the cadet or officer has left active duty.

Military personnel develop a sense of collective identity and an internal organisation system, to which is added an autonomous administration that implies the application of a body of ethical norms and performance guidelines. In the military profession there are three essential elements: technical specialisation, responsibility and corporate sense. This high degree of institutional autonomy to select the members of the naval elite that will lead the force, makes the analysis of the selection procedures and results even more relevant. For many years the institution enjoyed a low factual incidence of heteronomous political control in this process, a factor that generates and reinforces the great institutional cohesion that can be observed within itself. Similarly to other organisations – which determine the selection and promotion of the elites within the service – it consolidates patterns of behaviour and thought, while generating supporters and links. These features are particularly notable in a profession whose development is carried out exclusively within the organisation.

Officer training is not exhausted at the Naval Academy, where they graduate as midshipmen and a degree in naval systems, but after two years in operational destinations and upon promotion to sub lieutenant all officers must take a year course at the Naval Officers School (ESOA) where they perform a basic technical training course to obtain any of the following specialisations: artillery, underwater-weapons, propulsion or communications. After a period of between six and nine years of service, and with the rank of first lieutenant in the last year, they will return to this same school where they must take the so-called Application Course that also lasts one year and will allow them to acquire tactical training in order to be qualified to perform as an assistant staff officer. This qualifies the naval officer, for example, to stand watch in the combat information centre (CIC), that is, the nerve centre of any warship.

The cruiser *Buenos Aires*, at the time of its commission was considered the fastest ship in Latin America. (Author's Collection)

Future naval aviators carry out a basic training course in Punta Indio, in the province of Buenos Aires, and future submariners at the Submarine School based in Mar del Plata, where they must pass the rigorous academic, physical and practical exams to be admitted to these branches of the Navy.

These specialisations – surface officers, naval aviators, marines and submariners – represent the subcultural dimension of the officer corps, and although there is a healthy competition between each branch, it never shows to outsiders.

In the Argentine Navy, those who command the warships see themselves as the legitimate heirs of Admiral Brown and are proud to differentiate themselves from the rest. Submariners also consider themselves an elite group, as they firmly argue that submarines are the quintessential offensive weapon in any fleet worth its salt. The aviators, on the other hand, have identical arguments in order to the merit of their specialisation and perhaps they are those who emerged from the Malvinas conflict with greater prestige within the service;

The Type 42 guided missile destroyer ARA *Hercules* (hull number D-1, displacement 4,100 tonnes) built in the UK, at Barrow-in-Furness. On service entry in 1977 it was by far the most modern ship of the Argentine fleet. (Argentine Navy)

after all they went down in history with the resonant sinking of the Type 42 destroyer HMS *Sheffield*, the Type 21 frigate HMS *Ardent* and the very important logistics ship SS *Atlantic Conveyor*. All these strikes have been the object of multiple analyses by all the world´s navies, including those of Great Britain and the United States. Regardless of the specialisation, the professional values of all officers are unquestionable, although there are differences in the primacy of one or another branch within the service. Notwithstanding this, each subculture receives the same training in naval strategy and operational strategy at the Naval War College. However, there is no doubt that the combat platform with which the naval officer will go to war to fight will mark his way of thinking especially at the tactical level.

Concerning personal values, experience shows that – in most cases – they are also very homogeneous regardless of the officer´s years of service and naval career. All those who at some point have served in the navy reflect – to a greater or lesser extent – the powerful influence of the values instilled in them by the institution.

The naval career is very itinerant as it can include not only operational posts such as warships, aircraft or submarine squadrons, but training schools abroad, the Military House at the Presidency or the Ministry of Defence, and even diplomatic appointments as naval attaché in Argentine embassies in different countries. That is why it is very important for naval officers to know the rules that will enable them to move on towards the higher ranks of the institution. The qualification and selection system for promotion in the Argentine Navy is a key element on the issue of *military autonomy*. This refers to the mechanisms and freedom of action that the service has to determine which of its officers will eventually lead the institution and make the most important decisions.

The career of a regular naval officer is supervised by senior officers who make up the so-called JAP (Permanent Advisory Board) and two other instances where the officer is evaluated by both qualification boards. The board is a rigorous selection process that is composed by the so-called *informants*, who examine the performance of the officer and evaluate the candidate's future appointments, depending on availability and the professional and personal merits of the candidate. Among the topics examined it can be mentioned: his intellectual conditions, discipline, competence in his operational training, competence in his specialty, leadership qualities, aptitude for command and so forth.

Those officers who by merit and seniority are eligible for promotion, also undergo a rigorous selection process analogous to the above mentioned, where at the highest point of the rank pyramid – superior officers – plays the interaction that occurs between the service and the politicians who run the government, who are constitutionally and politically called to exercise control over the armed forces.

Argentina´s Constitution establishes that the President is the Commander-in-Chief of the Armed Forces[33] and who selects the superior officers of the service – captains and admirals – with the agreement of the Senate. In recent years, the Executive has deviated from the proposals for promotion made by the Navy; this has generated a conflictive context within a navy that year after year has fewer appointments to distribute, given the lack of new acquisitions in terms of naval platforms and the frequent budget cuts to which the armed forces are currently subject. Finally, it should be noted that the flag officers are promoted by the President of the Republic himself with Congress's approval, and as a symbol of their flag rank status they are given a sword, which imitates that used by Admiral William Brown.

Institutional Culture and Strategic Culture

The decision-making process in matters of defence, is not an abstract construct based purely in the present moment but is, rather, steeped in the beliefs, biases, traditions and cultural identity of the individual country – all of which feed into its strategic culture.

The concept of strategic culture dates from the 1970s, when American political scientist Jack Snyder introduced the term to explain the strategy of the Soviet Union. Snyder warned of the dangers of assuming that the Soviets would have the same set of values and beliefs as the US strategic community. Crucially, Snyder challenged the view that the Soviets would play the same nuclear war game as the US, as existing generic rational actor paradigms and game theoretical modelling suggested. As part of his critique, Snyder promoted a form of analysis of Soviet behaviour and strategic thinking which could take more fully into account the particular Soviet historical experiences of war which, he argued, shaped Moscow´s perspectives on contemporary security issues. Subsequently, he saw that a unique Soviet strategic culture had developed through a particular historical process, forming a perception prism through which strategy issues were viewed by Soviet decision makers. This pattern affected policy by setting the parameters of national debates and consequently guided and shaped policy choices.

In Argentina during the military regime – also known for the Spanish word *Junta* – this did not apply: all decisions related to naval strategy were made by the Commander-in-Chief, as head of the Navy and member of the ruling group.

Institutional culture and strategic culture are quite different concepts. The former concerns culture in a specific sense within very narrow parameters – that of a military institution – whereas the latter considers culture from a broader perspective that includes all aspects of the state.

A Cultural Fracture: the Falklands/Malvinas War

Contrary to what is generally thought, neither the institutional culture of the service nor the strategic culture of the country had anything to do with the crisis-management process that ultimately led to the Falklands/Malvinas War. The reason behind this abrupt change in foreign policy by Argentina lies elsewhere. An appropriate starting point is the work of Sir James Cable, which captures the key elements to consider. In September 1982 he wrote:

> One of the most interesting questions for a historian of the future will be to know exactly when, after 1966, Argentina changed its policy of the force of reason, for a policy of the argument of force … There is no evidence that any person in Argentina expected a war … [34]

As this distinguished author correctly assessed nobody in Argentina expected a war over the Falkland/Malvinas Islands, least of all the Argentine Navy. Practically all the officer corps, including many senior naval officers on active duty, came to know of Operation Azul by reading about it in the newspapers on 2 April. Commander Fernando Azcueta, CO of the submarine ARA *San Luis* – who was later expected to cause havoc among the enemy fleet – heard the news on the radio. Even Admiral Anaya´s youngest son Guillermo – at the time an Army lieutenant who served as a helicopter pilot – denies advance knowledge of the Falklands operation. Is this the pattern of a country that is about to go to war with a major world power? Certainly not.

Royal Marines surrender to Argentine forces on 2 April 1982 after a symbolic fight at Government House. (Photo by Rafael Wollmann)

the US posture in Central America and would mean a diplomatic setback in the Southern Cone countries.

Then why did Argentina invade the Falkland/Malvinas in 1982? This can only be rationally explained through the unique role of Admiral Anaya who had a fixed idea on the Falklands/Malvinas issue since he was a junior officer. In terms of decision-making style, Anaya and General Galtieri operated on their own, and when – finally – a decision to capture the islands or not had to be taken, it was done with the minimum of fuss and maximum secrecy.

Anaya was born in Bahia Blanca on 27 September 1926; he owed his military career to his father, a physician born in Bolivia. After graduating as an MD in Argentina, where he specialised in urology, he worked briefly in the city of Dolores, a small town located in the province of Buenos Aires. Later he settled permanently in the city of Bahia Blanca, which offered greater possibilities of progress and was the trade centre of the region. Among Anaya´s father´s patients were General Manni, at the time CO of the 5th Army Corps stationed near Bahia Blanca. It was this friend of the family who recommended Dr Anaya to send his son to the General San Martin Military Academy, a high school of elite pupils that enjoyed high prestige. Anaya entered with the class of 1940, along with the future General Galtieri. At that time, with the second year passed, the cadets could be admitted into the Air Force Academy – still under the Argentine Army – without taking an admission exam. The young Anaya fervently wished to be an aviator, but his parents refused to give their consent to such an idea. Only then did Anaya turn his attention to the Navy. He was admitted at the Naval Academy on 26 January 1944. Four years later he graduated with honours, second out of a total of 87 midshipmen, behind the future Vice Admiral Carlos Castro Madero, a very distinguished flag officer that chaired for many years the strategic National Commission of Nuclear Energy.[36]

By 1982 Anaya´s hard, shut-in personality, had made him reach the pinnacle of his naval career at age 56. Within the service he was reputed to be a 'strict disciplinarian, deeply dedicated to his profession'.[37] During his long and distinguished naval career, he had been in command of several surface units and had occupied important operational postings. He had served as naval attaché in the United Kingdom and had been in charge of the Argentine Naval Commission in Europe. He later attended to the Ecole Superieure de Guerre or War College in Paris, where he became a fervent admirer of Charles De Gaulle and surely acquired his notorious dislike for England.[38] It is well known that his thesis at the Argentine Naval War College was about a plan to occupy the Falkland/Malvinas Islands – the original paper has disappeared from the Navy´s archives. We also know that during 1977 – when in command of the fleet as a Rear Admiral – he had prepared a memo addressed to Admiral

This was the making of a leading figure within the triumvirate of the three commanders-in-chief of the armed forces. That leading figure, the late Admiral Jorge Isaac Anaya, C-in-C of the Argentine Navy, was the warlord who thought he could take the Falkland/Malvinas Islands and get away with it without a fight and without altering significantly the fragile balance of power that existed in Latin America. Soft-spoken, sterner and more timid than the regular naval officers, he actually had never wanted a war with the United Kingdom. He wanted greater power, greater prestige for the military – and above all more authority in Latin American affairs for Argentina – but he preferred to obtain them by frightening rather than fighting Great Britain. He wanted the gladiator´s rewards without the battle, and whenever the prospect of battle came too close, he shrank. The decision of the Junta to resort to force constituted a totally anomalous and unexpected phenomenon.

By January 1982 the relations between Argentina and the local population of the Falkland/Malvinas Islands had never been better. The Communications Agreement of 1971 provided the introduction of a weekly air service with the mainland. The integration between the continent and the island had consolidated in the decade that followed to a point that the new governor – Rex Hunt – had given his consent to build a new residence for the Argentine representative, second only in dimensions and importance to that of the British governor, also known as Government House.[35]

All the evidence suggests that there was no political or military need to resolve the Malvinas issue in 1982. With hindsight it seems clear that this was not the best time to escalate a conflict with Britain, especially when 149 years had elapsed since the beginning of the dispute and nothing presupposed the existence of impediments to await a more favourable opportunity.

Furthermore, by December 1981 there was an extraordinary agreement of interests between Argentina, the United Kingdom and the United States. None of the three countries had anything to gain by a conflict between them. An armed conflict would be a contrary move for Washington as it sought to secure South America behind

Emilio Eduardo Massera, where he proposed to take the Falkland/Malvinas Islands by force.[39] In other words: he did all he could during his naval career to persuade his superiors to do something about the Falklands/Malvinas issue, but had failed every time thanks to the prevailing Argentine strategic culture that dictated a more pragmatic approach to solve foreign policy matters.

The US Secretary of State, Alexander Haig, talks with President Leopoldo Galtieri and Foreign Minister Nicanor Costa Méndez in the Casa Rosada. By his side former US General Vernon Walters follows the conversation. (Photo by Cdr Roberto Salinas)

In 1978 Anaya left the fleet to occupy the position of Director of Naval Personnel. In 1980, as vice admiral, he was appointed Chief of the General Staff of the Navy – virtually number 2 of the service – which he held until Armando Lambruschini – fellow naval academy class graduate and friend of Admiral Massera – retired and chose him as his successor. According to Lombardo 'it is possible that Massera was an important factor in this decision'[40] since the two natural candidates to occupy that post out of prestige and career – Admirals Edgardo Segura and Humberto Barbuzzi – unexpectedly asked for their early retirement in 1980.

On 11 September 1981 Anaya – now with the rank of full admiral – took command of the Navy and became a member of the ruling Junta. The opportunity he had waited for so long had come at last. He immediately started to make the necessary arrangements that would allow him to carry out his personal – not institutional – lifelong desire: to recover the Falkland/Malvinas Islands.

Lieutenant General Roberto Eduardo Viola succeeded General Videla in the presidency of the nation, thus integrating the second ruling Junta. General Leopoldo Fortunato Galtieri – an engineer officer that resembled the American actor George C. Scott in his role of General Patton's movie namesake – had been in command of the Army since December 1979, despite being one of the last in his class at the Military Academy, and even having to re-attend a year at the Army War College. Galtieri reached that high hierarchy thanks to Viola's support, who erroneously considered him a man without political ambitions. Taking advantage of this vote of confidence of his former superior officer and mentor, Galtieri dedicated himself to dismantle systematically the influence of Viola in the Army and achieved it in just 16 months, benefiting from the latter's political mistakes during his brief administration.

Galtieri and Anaya criticised General Viola's inaction and misgivings, whose administration was also affected by a regional economic crisis. But at that time the critical situation that the country was going through was blamed on Viola, embodied in his much-disapproved Minister of Economy, Lorenzo Sigaut. These causes were publicly invoked to precipitate his fall from power, but when he was asked to resign, Viola rejected to do so. This left no other alternative to the Junta than to order his relief on 11 December 1981, claiming "health reasons". Galtieri had now the support of the Navy to overthrow his predecessor and at the same time retain the command of the Army.[41]

Some authors argue that the acceleration of the coup against Viola suggests the urgency to carry out the Falklands/Malvinas landing promoted by Anaya. It is alleged that Anaya convinced Galtieri that he would be the political beneficiary of the operation, which in turn would allow him to be elected president for the 1984-1990 term.[42]

In line with his plan, the Argentine naval attaché in London, Captain Gualter Allara, was instructed to consult the Argentine ambassador there (Carlos Ortiz de Rozas) with regard to the event of a military takeover of the Falkland/Malvinas Islands without loss of life. Anaya´s lack of confidence in Argentine diplomacy made him propose Rear Admiral (Retired) Rodolfo Luchetta – Anaya´s personal friend – to replace Ortiz de Rozas, on the grounds that Luchetta – who had recently served as naval attaché in London – retained important political contacts that would be useful to get a go ahead from the British. Eventually, Luchetta's designation was dropped and instead he was appointed ambassador to Italy.[43] Anaya finally changed his mind when Foreign Minister Nicanor Costa Méndez assured him that Ortiz de Rozas not only supported the Falklands/Malvinas operation, but that there would be no fear of a military reaction from the United Kingdom – as long as English bloodshed was avoided.[44]

Anaya's influence on President Galtieri was growing. They were good friends; they knew and respected each other since they were school mates. The usual inter-service rivalry that until then had significantly hindered the acts of government, in one way or another, suddenly disappeared. This friendship and mutual trust between them greatly contributed to how future events would unfold.

In foreign policy the new ruling Junta was now advised by intelligent, sophisticated civilian and fervent Anglophile Nicanor Costa Méndez, a prestigious lawyer with an impeccable résumé, who limped and walked aided by a walking stick. The new Foreign

Minister had important connections in political and military circles and had already occupied the same post during the government of General Juan Carlos Ongania (1966-1970). Everything suggests that he was aware of the Junta´s intentions to recover the Falkland/Malvinas Islands by force.

A revealing testimony by Bonifacio del Carril (1911-1994), former Foreign Minister of President José Maria Guido, tells us how the Junta manipulated the South Georgia incident to trigger the Falklands/Malvinas crisis. The prestigious historian, distinguished lawyer and close friend of Costa Méndez says:

> I do not have all the conversations written down. But on 29 or 30 March, Costa Méndez informed me about the courses of action that were being studied in the face of the demand made by the British government for Argentina to evict the Argentine metal workers [Davidoff scrap metal dealers who had landed in Leith Harbour, South Georgia]. I told him then that, in my opinion, if the decision to take advantage of the incident of the metal dealers to recover the [Falklands/] Malvinas was final, the most convenient thing for Argentina was to let the British evict them by force. The important thing was to have an act of force executed by the British as an initial act [of aggression] and not just a simple threat. I pointed out, on the other hand, that British military superiority was overwhelming and that in the economic field, Great Britain could exercise strong sanctions against Argentina, because, despite the decline of the empire, England remained one of the most important financial centres in the world. He [Costa Méndez] told me that it was very difficult for England to react militarily because of the high cost of the operation, that the Armed Forces had made all necessary contingency plans to neutralise any attempt, and that he was going to have at least three weeks before the British arrived to the [Falklands/] Malvinas Islands.[45]

Indeed, on 20 March 1982, the British government dispatched the polar ship HMS *Endurance* with Royal Marines in order to evict by force the Argentine workers who had landed at Leith Harbour in South Georgia. This was the key moment that would trigger the conflict and that the Junta described as *ultimatum*, in order to escalate the conflict and thus justify – in the face of public opinion – the planned recovery of the archipelago.

According to Anaya:

> Accepting that the workers be evicted by force or force them to recognise a foreigner's status and continue negotiating with Great Britain caused the Argentine position to lose credibility and strength in future negotiations, as well as weaken our claims regarding the rights permanently sustained by our country. This would bring a great loss of prestige by not reacting with energy to an attitude that affected national honour and dignity [*sic*].[46]

None of this is true. There were other options open to the Junta that were perfectly viable, but were deliberately set aside, such as: a) evacuating the Argentine workers with a Navy transport – to reduce tension and prevent Britain from escalating the dispute – and b) not evacuate them and let England execute an act of force against Argentine nationals; such an incident could have been exploited by Argentina to gain international support in multilateral forums.

Anaya – prone to impulsive decisions – adopted a course of action consistent with his plan. He dispatched the polar ship ARA *Bahía Paraiso* that conveniently had on board a group of 12 amphibious commandos, with small-arms, commanded by Lieutenant Alfredo Astiz, which landed in Leith Harbour on the night of 24 March with orders to avoid the eviction of the Argentine workers. The presence of tactical divers aboard the *Bahía Paraiso* reveals the intent of the Junta to escalate the conflict, as such personnel were not part of the regular ship's company, whose priority at that time was to disembark the families that would stay that winter at the Antarctic Naval Base Esperanza and re-embark the personnel of the construction battalion that had completed a new building for the Orcadas naval detachment.[47]

Consequently, the South Georgia incident should have been overcome through diplomatic channels and avoided at all costs. This suggested course of action did not offer complications of any kind that could affect national honour and dignity; instead, it was used as a convenient excuse to advance the Falklands/Malvinas operation. This advance was not only counterproductive for the Argentine forces – who were not ready to engage in a conventional war against a major naval power – but also benefited the enemy to a greater extent.[48]

In that context, the occupation of the Falkland/Malvinas Islands with the purpose of being in a better position to negotiate, concluded in a military escalation. This shows that the Junta was not in a position to control the events or measure the likely British reaction. This naïve scenario – which to some extent had great popular support – made it an unprecedented military adventure for Argentina where the country had everything to lose and nothing to gain in the event of a conventional military conflict, especially when the British military reaction became a reality, and no diplomatic alternatives had been taken to neutralise it.

Much has been speculated in the literature about the reasons that led Anaya and Galtieri to take this course of action. It is almost undeniable, however, that if the Galtieri administration had enjoyed good internal economic and political health, it would hardly have embarked the country in this adventure. The – perhaps not exclusive – role of internal politics in this decision is thus practically irrefutable, regardless of the other considerations that the case may deserve. The government gained – temporarily – great apparent popularity, as it had endorsed a popular cause.[49]

Anaya himself admitted that his role before, during and after the Falklands/Malvinas War was essentially political and not military, so it was in that capacity that he concluded that 'the British aggression confronted us with a necessary war to defend our rights'.[50] This assessment was – as later demonstrated – nonsense, and subordinated the future of the country and its armed forces to a utopian political objective, on false premises that responded to a naïve understanding of international relations and a gross lack of knowledge of the enemy's capabilities.

Indeed, to the great disappointment of those responsible, the United States opted – in the emergency – to support its former and solid ally, the United Kingdom, rather than what it was perceived as an adventurous military regime with little foreseeable behaviour. Obviously, Argentine cooperation in Central America was not enough to alter a traditional alliance order.

Nevertheless, the Junta made a good job maintaining the Falklands/Malvinas operation a secret. Only a very small group of senior officers knew of its existence. The Navy in particular was kept in the dark to the very last moment, and everything was done without the knowledge of the officer corps.

In this context, it seems clear that there was a fracture in the institutional culture of the Navy, because Admiral Anaya acted on his own, under the veil of his executive post as a member of the military Junta, leaving aside the Council of Admirals (permanent advice

The late Vice Admiral (retired) Juan José Lombardo (left) with the author, around 2002, in his country house in Lujan, Buenos Aires Province. (Author's collection)

body to the C-in-C), the Joint Chiefs of Staff, and his subordinate admirals who had no intervention whatsoever in that decision. The reasons for this anomalous conduct – considering that the country was going to engage in a war with the third naval power in the world – seem to have been four: a) to keep the operation a military secret, b) the surely negative view of his subordinate admirals to undertake a military adventure for which the Navy was not prepared, c) the erroneous advice of the civil servants of the Foreign Ministry in the sense that a British military reaction should not be feared in the case of recovering the islands, and d) that the US government would remain neutral.

As we have already discussed no such scenario existed in the Navy before mid-December 1981. Additionally – as stated by Admiral Lombardo – although the extreme crisis with Chile that had occurred in the final months of 1978 had been overcome, the general mood in the armed forces was far from having settled down over that issue, and at the time, this was a paramount concern in the minds of the officer corps. These simple facts allow us to conclude that Anaya's gamble to resolve the sovereignty dispute over the Falkland/Malvinas Islands by the use of limited military force is not consistent with the prevailing institutional culture in the service at the time, and suggests that any other naval officer in that same position would not have made that fatal decision – and would refrain to do so in the future.[51]

2
CULTURE, STRATEGY AND THE FALKLANDS/MALVINAS CONFLICT

In the early 1980s the Argentine Navy was adjusting herself to the new combat systems provided by no other than the third most powerful naval force in the world: the Royal Navy. Indeed, the contracts signed in March 1969 between the Argentine Navy and Vickers Ltd, the British shipbuilders at Barrow-in-Furness for the construction of a Type 42 guided missile destroyer, and the technical assistance to build a second unit in Argentine shipyards, together with a new WG13 Sea Lynx high performance helicopter for each ship, and other military cooperation programmes that linked both navies are conclusive proof that the institutional culture of the Argentine Navy in this period was aimed at acquiring an important part of the combat doctrine of the Royal Navy.

Argentine naval strategy had become heavily oriented to become an ASW force due to the role assigned to Latin American navies by the US at the height of the Cold War. However, this role failed to recognise the existence of an underlying philosophy towards naval strategy which favoured a more flexible role. Consequently, no significant changes were made in the strategic outlook of the service. Limited sea control strategies and the maintenance of a broad spectrum of capabilities for maritime forces was the preferred scenario at this time. The dominance of surface ships within the Argentine Navy reflected the cultural preferences of the institution towards this type of warfare.

At the time, the entire Argentine armed forces were fixed on Chile, with regard to the Beagle Channel dispute – nobody thought of the United Kingdom as a potential enemy. Yet, it is true that during 1978 a top-secret memorandum written by Admiral Emilio Eduardo Massera, Commander-in-Chief of the Navy, reached the presidency – held at the time by General Videla – proposing to retake the Falkland/Malvinas Islands by force, but the idea was rapidly dropped by the ruling Junta when the Navy failed to come up with the alleged plans of the operation.[1]

However, four years later, with the appointment of the obscure figure of Admiral Jorge Isaac Anaya as head of the Argentine Navy – and new member of the ruling Junta – the plan to recapture the Falklands/Malvinas was reassessed by the military government once again. This implied an unprecedented *cultural fracture* within the Navy, because the scheme was carried out without the knowledge of

Sea Lynx helicopter 0735/3-H142 operated from ARA *Hercules*. (Argentine Navy Photo)

the officer corps. Indeed, this unexpected departure from the current institutional culture would bring a very fragile South American nation, with no experience in war, to challenge Great Britain – still a major world power – to a clash which neither of them wanted.

Anaya – artificer of the idea – convinced the Junta to go ahead with Operation Azul – later renamed Rosario – a decision that would put the Argentine Navy on a collision course with a much respected and friendly navy who had been training its naval personnel and updating its naval platforms during the previous decade. This formidable enemy was at the time devoted to planning and preparing for the Third Battle of the Atlantic against the Soviet Union. This single threat and single scenario were forced on the Royal Navy by the political necessity to justify their continued existence in terms of their contribution to the Atlantic Alliance´s strategy. This had the unfortunate result of eroding the flexibility, versatility and autonomous capability of the Royal Navy and of gradually reducing it to the auxiliary role of a specialised ASW force.[2] This strategic outlook was about to change thanks to the personal – not institutional – ambition of a man that did not represent in any way the Argentine Navy´s culture.

This unorthodox approach to a very sensitive domestic issue without proper institutional backup left all combat units of the Argentine Navy literally in the dark in regard to the coming Malvinas operation. Only a very small group of high-ranking officers within the service knew of the plan, and these men failed to give sound advice on the ill-fated operation, convinced that Britain would not, and could not, mount a military response sufficient to dislodge Argentine troops without unacceptable military losses. Furthermore, the Junta failed to recognise that Argentina did not possess the international standing to back up such a bold move, nor could they count on any major ally of medium-strength that would make England hesitate before committing itself to a limited war, even on an issue which affected no vital British interest.

Argentine Navy Culture and Naval Strategy

Strategic culture – a term coined in 1977 in the context of the US-Soviet strategic nuclear confrontation – is the result of beliefs, values and traditions regarding, how, when and why to wage war. These notions vary from nation to nation. Every nation has a unique combination of geographical setting, historical experience and political culture which shapes the formation of beliefs about the use of force. These beliefs persist over time and in turn influence the strategic behaviour of the nation.[3] In other words, military cultures generate distinctive styles in terms of strategy. Each culture will create a particular style of warfare.

The Falklands/Malvinas War was the first major naval engagement for the Argentine Navy in 120 years. When the British asked themselves what style of warfare an enemy such as the rather tiny and virgin Argentine Navy would display, they naturally underestimated their foe, relying on *Jane´s Fighting Ships* and all sorts of generalisations. However, there was no straightforward answer to that question, given the country´s geographical setting – Latin America – a geopolitically isolated and low conflict zone, whose traditional threats normally came from Brazil or Chile.

In spite of the close association between both navies for over a decade prior to the South Atlantic conflict, the British had very little information regarding Argentina´s style of warfare or her strategic culture. The British – in general – displayed a lack of interest towards an implausible enemy, considered all in all inferior. This lack of cultural information blocked the Royal Navy´s ability to predict the intentions of their new foe. This should come as no surprise to anyone. Even in the hypothesis of having identified Argentina´s key strategic beliefs, to assess their impact upon policy was not a straightforward thing, for various other factors came into play, such as financial constraints or the actions of other states. After all, as Allan Macmillan points out, 'beliefs and attitudes … cannot be directly observed. Their existence and content have to be inferred from (many) sources such as strategic behaviour, writings and military manuals.'[4] That's why strategic culture analysis is so difficult to assess, and – most of the time – misleading.

Argentine Political Culture

A brief examination of the impact of Argentine political culture on its defence policy is pertinent to illustrate some of the points discussed in this chapter. An appropriate starting point is the work of Dr Carlos Escudé, a well-known Argentine expert in Political Science, whose book *Argentina: ¿Paria Internacional?* is very eloquent in describing how a first stage of a very successful foreign policy that extended to about 1940, turned into a second stage of great failure towards the 1950s:

> As demonstrated in *Gran Bretaña, Estados Unidos y la declinación Argentina 1942-1949*,[5] the transition from success to failure was due, fundamentally, but not exclusively, to the global changes in international relations, following the Second World War, namely: 1) The dismemberment of the British Empire, 2) The American hegemony in the West, and 3) The bipolar structure of the world that replaced its former multipolar structure.

> Until 1940 the Argentine national interest was so clear that all governments of the most distinct signs accepted that Argentina's first priority … and therefore its main objective in terms of foreign policy … was the defence of the insertion of the country in the world.
>
> Since 1950, after the shift [in foreign policy] had occurred, there is no concrete priority that can be described as consensual … The confusion and bewilderment generated by the displacement of Argentina from its traditional insertion in the world during the 1940s were of such dimensions, however, that the impossibility to replace the old Argentine diplomatic tradition with a new set of guidelines that would maximise a national interest, which had become blurred, should be deemed natural and almost necessary. Finally, in 1982, the confusion reached its paroxysm and the crisis at its most dramatic stage.
>
> A military government, the third in a process that rapidly lost all sustainability in civil society, joined the North American sphere in an unprecedented way for Argentine foreign policy, that is by actively cooperating with North American policy in Central America, incurring in this way, in an extreme westernism (in the post-war sense, that is, alignment with the US) never before subscribed by Argentine foreign policy.[6]

That is why Argentina´s defence policy up to 1981 was guided more or less by the idea of fulfilling a deterrent and contention role in the Southern Cone, preventing an alliance between neighbour countries that could threaten her security in military terms. This conception was originated in the confidence of the superiority that granted the weight of her economy and its greater relative development.

Regarding the international scenario, Argentina did not perceive direct threats to its security and maintained a pacifist position, tending towards neutrality. Almost at the end of Second World War, the pro-Allied neutrality was interrupted by the *coup d' état* of 1943, which retained its sympathies for the Axis powers bringing the country to international isolation. During the Cold War, Argentina maintained a pro-Western position, although it tried to avoid the intervention of the superpowers.

According to Carlos Escudé´s analysis on Argentine political culture:

> In recent decades, political measures sponsored by Argentine nationalism have tended, in practice, to diminish the power of the nation because an exaggerated perception of national power (or a misperception about which elements grant power in the twentieth century) has led us to try the impossible and, therefore, to resounding failures. Naïve nationalism was one of the factors – not the only one – that led to the loss of the traditional international insertion of this country during the 1940s. It helped to marginalize[*sic*] Argentina from alliances and markets. It led to the violation of international law, and launched the country into a wild war adventure [in reference to the 1982 conflict].[7]

During the Argentine de facto administrations of 1976-1982 the military misread the direction the world was heading, and what role Argentina had in it. Thus, they were unable to assess the poor strategic significance of Argentina in the eyes of the major world powers. Instead, the members of the ruling Junta were much more concerned with their personal roles in domestic issues and that of the service they represented. Unfortunately, the post-war period did not prove any better, and exposed the faulty democratic system of the country through different populist Peronist administrations which lacked a clear knowledge of what role Argentina should have in the new world order, all of which has led to a geopolitical chaos in terms of foreign policy.

Argentine Navy Culture

The first modern Argentine fleet (1874) known as Sarmiento´s Squadron after President Domingo Faustino Sarmiento – the first politician who saw the need to create a naval academy for a regular navy officer corps – was a brown-water navy acquired to protect the city of Buenos Aires and the River Plate estuary from a foreign blockade. But, as French strategist Andre Beaufre cautioned: 'The defensive can only pay if it leads sooner or later to a resumption of the initiative, in other words to some offensive action. A counter offensive is essential if submission to the will of the opponent is to be avoided.'[8]

Indeed, the Argentine Navy was well aware that taking offensive action is necessary to win battles at sea. The offensive is all about seizing, retaining and exploiting the initiative. This is effected by the acquisition of powerful offensive weapons and by ensuring that one maintains freedom of action to deploy and employ them. This means to use the Navy for offensive power projection operations. An institutional culture that encompasses this offensive approach leads to a tradition based on great victories in battles and campaigns at sea, fostering high *esprit de corps* and self confidence in the service.

However, it was very problematic for a third-world country such as Argentina – which at critical historic moments displayed an erratic foreign policy – to get modern weapon systems on the world market in order to fulfil the offensive spirit which its admirals demanded from time to time.

Indeed, Argentine neutrality during Second World War had serious consequences for the Navy, since after the Japanese attack on Pearl Harbour, Uruguay and Brazil turned decidedly in favour of the Allied cause, while Argentina remained neutral, a position that was interpreted as anti-American. This led to Argentina being left out of the Lend-Lease programme promoted by the United States. This was of great importance not only for the military but also in the subsequent economic output of friendly Latin American nations. This economic aid allowed Brazil to receive two-thirds of the funds sent by the US government to Latin America. This material help enabled them to become the first military power of the subcontinent.[9]

In spite of this, Argentina remained stubbornly adhered to its policy of neutrality. This worsened after the military coup of June 1943 – after which Argentina became an open supporter of the Axis powers – thus being the target of strong American political pressure until, near the end of the war, a confidential agreement was reached with the US government through which Argentina agreed to enter the war a few days before the cessation of hostilities.[10]

Consequently, Argentina´s naval forces not only lost the opportunity to update its combat platforms, doctrine and training at sea but also, from then on, they were deprived of a powerful maritime deterrent force, which had so effectively acted in support of their foreign policy during the last 80 years.[11]

This scenario was not new for the Navy; on different occasions during its long history the Naval Ministry had tried to get fresh funds to update its naval platforms without success. For example, in July 1925 a bill was passed to Congress in order to renew the Navy´s surface forces and acquire the first generation of three Argentine submarines. Admiral Manuel Domecq Garcia – then in charge – argued that:

> It is not possible to keep the Navy in the situation it has reached today, it is the duty of patriotism to begin as soon as possible the renewal of our surface forces that have been disappearing due to the fact that there has not been a coordinated and harmonious programme for its development to be followed, since the [new] acquisitions have almost always been done under the pressure of circumstances, and they have not been in agreement with the logic of a progressive armament programme that should guide the Armed Forces. The lessons collected after the [Great] War have made it necessary not only to modernise these last units, but also think about the acquisition of new weapons, such as [naval] aviation and the submarine, which have fundamentally changed the tactical factors of the organisation … The defence of the two great commercial roads of the Rio de la Plata and Bahía Blanca requires an efficient submarine service; these first boats that are requested and which are to be based at Mar del Plata are for submarine training purposes and will allow to gain experience and study the essential problems of our defence for the future.[12]

This lack of access to modern technology was not only a financial problem but was also directly related to the international context, particularly US-Soviet balance of power considerations, after the end of the Second World War.

It is interesting to note how low a priority has been traditionally awarded to the South American region. A poignant example is provided by almost all the literature on the value of the South Atlantic and South Pacific areas. When these are mentioned – and they were referred to only rarely before 1975 – the general gist of the theories always refers to the region outside the area marked by Article 4 of the Rio Treaty. The South Atlantic, thus – in universal appreciations – has a limited strategic value, and even this value is inferred to lie in the area nearest the African coast. In other words, the value of South America as such, or the implications of political and/or economic changes in South America, are *nil* on most world appraisals for defence, foreign or strategic studies.

British scholar Andrew Hurrell, writing about South Atlantic security, has said: 'The recent conflict between Britain and Argentina transformed the South Atlantic into an area of major international concern. It also underlined the extent to which the region has been generally neglected by both policymakers and academics.'[13] For Dr Hurrell, the policy of the US government toward Latin America has been as follows:

> For most of the post-war period the United States defence planning paid only slight attention to the South Atlantic region. Indeed, for Latin America as a whole, United States security doctrine assumed that the level of external threat to the area would remain low and that hemispheric solidarity behind Washington's leadership could be maintained. For these reasons the inter-American security system that emerged during and immediately after the end of the Second World War was a relatively loose one. Security relations were formalised in the Inter American Treaty of Reciprocal Assistance, or Rio Pact, signed in 1947, which has been supplemented over the years by bilateral military assistance treaties, and in the Charter of the Organisation of American States. Yet there has never been any kind of permanent military organisation. As Gordon Connell Smith points out, "The Inter-American Defence Board was established for political rather than military reasons." Subsequently, it has acquired no operational significance and has no forces under its direct command. Moreover, the two occasions when inter-American military measures have been taken – regarding Cuba and the Dominican Republic – served in many ways to impair the possibility of future cooperation and to underline Latin America concern that all inter-American defence arrangements could at least potentially be used by the US to further its hegemonic aspirations.[14]

This geopolitical context forced the Argentine Navy to adhere to an institutional culture which has normally been to avoid open war and adopt a defensive style of warfare due to her modest naval platforms, and a permanent low budget to operate a blue-water navy.

This approach to naval strategy is confirmed not only by the classic theorists on the subject – Sir Julian Corbett, Rear Admiral (USN), Alfred Thyer Mahan and many others – but also by the Argentine Navy's own servicemen. Such is the case of the late Captain (retired) José Maria Cohen, a well-known naval strategist within the officer corps and a distinguished professor of strategic studies at the Argentine Naval War College for many years. In 1972 he wrote: 'Without a doubt, we can affirm today that the principle that a war does not suit anyone is more valid than ever, since everything indicates that the only desired future for Latin America requires necessarily to opt for a loyal and generous understanding among all.'[15]

Reinforcing this statement further on he commented: 'The traditional policy of our country has been, is and will continue to be a pacifist one, because there is a firm conviction that in any conflict that may arise, the country must first exhaust all the Nation's resources before committing itself to an armed conflict.'[16]

The post-Second World War era was one of worldwide communist expansion. Indeed, the Cold War would be the answer to Argentina's prayers to update its naval platforms. The US strategy for the defence of the free world assigned Latin American navies the mission of ASW by the late 1950s.

In 1959 the US Chief of Naval Operations wrote to the Joint Chiefs of Staff: 'Hemispheric defence requires an ASW contribution by Latin American navies. This is a complicated type of naval warfare in which Latin America has little experience and in which they need US guidance and the United States needs their help.'[17]

That same year the chiefs of US naval missions in Latin America accompanied by a senior naval officer from each host nation, gathered in Panama for an annual conference. The Latin American officers recommended that their respective navies hold exercises with the US Navy on a regular basis. The result of this conference was a joint naval exercise called UNITAS (a Latin word that means unity). A US Navy Task Force composed of a few destroyers, a submarine or two, and some ASW aircraft was deployed each year to the South American continent to engage in naval exercises with friendly Latin American navies such as Argentina, emphasising ASW training. The exercises started in November-December 1960 (UNITAS I) and have continued – with brief interruptions – to the present day.

UNITAS promoted good will between fleets that were previously rivals, notably those of Argentina and Brazil, but could not bring together the navies of Argentina and Chile. It unified methods and doctrines used by Latin American navies, established English as the common operational language, and made NATO tactical manuals the rule books for exercises. Thus, it has contributed to the ability of Latin American navies to operate together.[18]

Complicating the UNITAS mission was the fact that in the 1960s Latin American navies did not possess the modern warships or technology to conduct modern ASW, the primary focus of UNITAS. Tactically, the success of such warfare is dependent on a superior

The Guppy-class submarine ARA *Santiago del Estero* (S-22) in dry dock in 1971. (Argentine Navy)

The submarine ARA *Santiago del Estero* (S-22) in her home port at Mar del Plata Naval Base, a very attractive city on the Argentine coast for summer holidays. (Argentine Navy Photo)

number of advanced aircraft and warships plus sophisticated sensor networks to overwhelm the subsurface opponent.

In spite of these shortcomings, during October and November 1962 the Argentine Navy participated with a division of two Fletcher-class destroyers, ARA *Rosales* (Commander Carlos Peralta) and ARA *Espora* (Commander Julio Vazquez) in Operation Quarantine during the Cuban Missile Crisis. The Argentine ships were under the overall command of Captain Constantino Arguelles. Operating from Chaguaramas Naval Base in Trinidad, they were part of a multinational Task Force led by Rear Admiral (USN) John A. Tyree. The Argentine ships made 86 patrols and intercepted 26 foreign merchant ships. Before returning to Argentina, they sailed a total of 12,500 nautical miles in international waters.

By the mid-1970s Latin American navies were still ill-equipped against the modern submarine. The prime ASW weapon available to the free world in 1974 was the ASROC system, and only two Latin American warships were armed with it: the Brazilian Gearing-class destroyers *Marcilio Dias* and *Mariz e Barros*. And, while the US Navy ascribed to Latin American navies a task requiring the most modern military hardware and weapons, American politicians opposed the transfer of sophisticated warfare systems. Additionally, some Latin American naval officers did not believe that the dominant mission of these navies should be solely ASW. Again, Captain José Maria Cohen of the Argentine Navy was one of them. He wrote:

> The Argentine Navy after WW II [*sic*], mainly because of USN material and publications, was evolving to become an ASW force only. But this "model" never was very attractive to us, even if we had no chance but to play the game as it was. The first important departure from this model was made in 1959 with the acquisition

Aircraft Carrier ARA *Independencia* during naval manoeuvres in the South Atlantic Ocean in 1963. (Argentine Navy)

In its attempt to reshape navies through warship transfers and exercises, the United States has offered educational opportunities to hundreds of Latin American officers at US naval facilities. By 1983, 185 officers had graduated from the command course at the Naval War College in Newport, Rhode Island. Of these, 95 have reached flag rank, 20 have become commanders-in-chief of their respective navies, and one has been a head of state. [20]

> of our first aircraft carrier (the *Independencia*) and our efforts (not very successful at the beginning) to get fighter bomber planes for it. I can´t say how this fact was perceived by the USN or the US Government, but I think I am not very far from the truth saying that they were not very happy, as it meant a clear departure from the role assigned in the "Inter-American" plans to our navy.[19]

Indeed, if one cares about prevailing in wartime, offensive forces are required. It is through the use of offensive capability, or the threat to employ it, that naval forces draw their leverage to shape political-military environments.

UNITAS – in its stress on ASW training – neglected surface, air and amphibious operations for years, something that was against the navy´s underlying philosophy. These aspects were somewhat reverted from 1981 onwards when UNITAS held its first amphibious exercise. As Scheina points out:

The purchase of an aircraft carrier with its air wing of attack aircraft gave the Argentine Navy offensive power projection. This offensive approach can be traced back to 1943 when an Executive Order (Decree 9006 16 September 1943) authorised the acquisition of two aircraft carriers. In the end only one was purchased, in July 1958 – the ARA *Independencia* – from the United Kingdom. This combat platform allowed for local and tactical offensives wherever and whenever enemy forces could be met. This particular aspect of the commonly adopted philosophy has hardly altered since the times of Admiral William Brown – father to the Argentine Navy – and continues to manifest itself in recent naval engagements such as the South Atlantic conflict.

Military strategy is about choices of how to apply military force among a variety of ways to achieve political objectives. Strategy seeks to foresee what a thinking, motivated, ruthless, clever, vicious adversary might do and then to craft ways to thwart it.[21] As R.W. Barnett points out, 'Only rarely is there a precise correlation between ends, ways and means. The normal situation is that means are limited, and struggles arise over choices either of ways to apply them or of objectives to be sought. Moreover, ways, means and ends are in constant interaction.'[22] Given the uniqueness of the maritime environment, naval strategy has always been highly complex.

Warfare in the maritime arena tends to be protracted, and for a host of reasons, including the global size of the battle-space and its potential to provide sanctuary, the relatively slow movements of waterborne platforms on and under the surface of the sea, the absence of geographical lines to organise and focus action, and the ability for oceanic naval forces to avoid conflict. In addition, the losses of capital ships, coupled with their low overall numbers, militates against employing them recklessly.[23]

A rare view of the carrier *Independencia* entering the port of Ushuaia in the southern tip of Argentina. Note the North American Texan AT-6 A aircraft on the stern section of the flight deck. (Argentine Navy)

'In view of these considerations' – wrote Roger Barnett – 'states have historically adopted six national strategies for the employment of their maritime forces: three offensively-oriented (fleet battle, blockade and maritime power projection) and three defensive in nature (commerce raiding, fleet-in-being and costal defence).'[24]

All of the strategies pivot on the central problem of naval warfare: finding the adversary. Surveillance and counter surveillance – finding and hiding – constitute the first order of business. The lone exception to this general rule is the fleet-in-being strategy, for the fleet-in-being wants its presence to be known and felt, but it does not seek battle.[25] Argentina's fleet has traditionally been small in terms of naval platforms, only capable of defensive and limited sea control operations; however, it has always retained a high degree of training. This was clearly reflected during the South Atlantic conflict.

Argentine Naval Strategy in the 1970s–1980s

In the early 1970s the naval balance of power in the Southern Cone in particular, showed that Argentine sea power – which had once allowed the country to deal with a combined threat from Brazil and Chile – had not only been completely shattered, but continued to turn rapidly against her. Brazil had initiated a programme to renew its naval forces that, due to its quantity, quality and pace of new acquisitions, evidenced the clear intention of Brazil to dominate the South Atlantic, placing Argentina on a clear inferiority level. Chile in turn had managed to incorporate some new units and modernise others. To face these potential enemies, the Argentine Navy had a worn-out and mostly obsolete naval force.

Argentina´s response to this critical situation was an Executive Order (Decree 956 "S" –for Secret – 28 March 1974) signed by President Juan Peron through which a National Plan for Military Naval Construction was authorised, which provided for the construction of a first series of warships (destroyers) of local construction with a displacement of 2,800 tons and a speed of 32 knots and a range at economic speed of 4,500 nautical miles. It was projected that these units would be built by the local AFNE shipyards in Rio Santiago under the supervision of the Navy and the assistance of foreign firms. For different reasons – mainly of a political nature – this plan never materialised and was ultimately replaced by a new one that was ordered by Executive Order – Decree 285 "S" 29 January 29 1979 – that authorised a contract with the German firm Blohm & Voss for the construction of four new multipurpose destroyers of the Almirante Brown-class (MEKO 360) of 2,900 tons and 30.5 knots of speed. These warships were finally commissioned between March 1983 and September 1984, too late for the Falklands/Malvinas conflict, and are currently the core of the Argentine battle fleet. These ships had important systems of British origin – they were originally to be equipped with Sea Lynx helicopters – that had to be replaced; this handicap conditioned their operational performance for years, especially their anti-submarine capability and the over-the-horizon target designation capacity, which was finally overcome with the acquisition in 1996 of the first four Fennec helicopters of French origin.

The progress of the Cold War during this period had no major impact on Argentine strategic thinking, although it did show a greater emphasis on anti-submarine operations as already discussed. The preferred technology for the Navy at this time continued to be predominantly the surface vessel: a clear reflection of the institutional preferences of the service over the most effective platform available: the submarine. This orientation was explicitly supported by the successive Commanders-in-Chief of the Navy.

In this regard, the role of the Argentine Navy in the event of war between the Soviet Union and the United States was mostly an extension of the functions of the Atlantic Alliance (NATO) around the defence of maritime traffic in the South Atlantic and of the trade routes to supply central Europe. For this purpose, the Argentine Navy participated in annual UNITAS exercises led by a US Navy Task Force between 1971 and 1981 where Argentina – shortly before the Falklands/Malvinas War – obtained excellent marks.

By the 1980s the Argentine Navy was comprised of four major elements: surface ships, submarines, aircraft and marine corps, a traditional hierarchy. Surface ships have a longer history of service to the institution than the other forms of combat platforms and represent the preferred technology. The philosophy of the Argentine Navy is inextricably linked to this quartet of capability, which in itself mirrors the essential nature of the so-called maritime battle-space.

It is an accepted principle that a balanced naval force offers flexible options ranging from the projection of naval power to amphibious warfare. Naval forces, due to their intrinsic characteristics of agility, mobility and relative independence, are an especially suitable instrument to make their presence felt and if necessary, they can formalise a threat and sustain it without performing a single act of war. They can be deployed on the high seas without any commitment, wait and gain time for diplomacy. If expectations are poor, ships are easy to regroup. Warships allow you to choose the best course of action, that is why – in a crisis power projection – capability is an important contributor to naval diplomacy. Naval forces are a flexible instrument. Additionally, the maritime conflict is much easier to limit and control than war on land and in the air, in addition to generating less collateral damage.

Argentine strategists such as Captain Cohen thought that a truly balanced naval force should comprise surface forces – the fleet – naval aviation, and amphibious forces. In this regard, he was of the opinion, for example, that it was not worth having a high-profile marine corps if there were not enough ships to transport, to protect or to land it on a beachhead.

The question of the balance of naval power was a serious problem for countries such as Argentina that had a tendency to assign many missions to their Navy but could not provide themselves with the means necessary to fulfil them.

The solution to the problem was simple: to reduce the number of missions assigned to the Navy and not to think in terms of any particular kind of war: a small country like Argentina must prepare for the most likely and most dangerous hypotheses, and those hypotheses must be perfectly defined and fully resolved. The problem today is about what conflict hypothesis to prepare for, said Cohen in 1979.[26]

On the other hand – in principle and far from being exhaustive – there is the need to protect the resources of the Argentine seas, immersed in a scenario of global exhaustion, and at the same time, the need to have the capacity to participate in expeditionary operations, which is the form of peace enforcement missions for which most of the countries in organisations such as the UN and NATO are being prepared. Argentina has already participated in a number of these missions, such as Haiti, Cyprus, West Sahara and the Middle East.

In any case, power projection requires surface forces. A capital ship creates an adequate impression of political will. Aircraft carriers are particularly suitable for this role, and their aircraft demonstrate a flexible presence in cases of a diplomatic crisis situation. Argentina acquired its first aircraft carrier, ARA *Independencia* (hull number V-1; former HMS *Warrior*) from the United Kingdom in July 1958 during the government of President Arturo Frondizi. This capital ship was replaced in October 1969 by ARA *25 de Mayo* (hull number V-2; former HMS *Venerable*). These ships conferred on the Navy the strategic ability to operate a fighter-bomber wing of combat aircraft, an advantage that no other South American country had until the mid-1990s. This placed the Argentine Navy in the select group of nations that operated capital units of this class.

The Argentine Navy of the 1980s was changing the existing force structures as well as the other Argentine armed forces. As Alastair Finlan rightly points out, 'Force structures represent more than just the visible physical expression of an armed service in support of the state´s posture on a security issue … in many cases … the force structure or the composition of the fleet expresses the underlying philosophy of the institution.'[27] The emphasis on the importance of surface vessels in the Argentine Navy stems from deeply rooted cultural preferences for such configurations.

It is clear that Argentine naval policy in 1980 was in a state of adapting to the new missile age but retained a large capability of surface ships that was significantly larger than its underwater platforms. This disproportion between surface forces and submarine vessels did not occur by accident; it reflected the institutional preferences of the service that had not changed substantially in the previous 30 years.

The parameters of Argentine naval strategy at this time had evolved from the experience of other navies in the First and Second World Wars, with a subsequent readjustment to new technology. Naval technology is complex because the environment is complex and difficult to master. Moreover, the risks and costs of failing either in weather or battle are ultimate.

In this context the best strategic variant for a small fleet of few high value units such as the Argentine Navy was the maintenance of a fleet-in-being: the possession of a fleet with no explicit intentions to engage the enemy in a decisive naval battle. It also constitutes – according to Julian Corbett – a valuable strategy that, intelligently used, can be very advantageous for a weaker navy. Indeed, these surface forces will always represent a threat to the enemy, even though their purpose is not to engage in combat with the adversary, unless a favourable opportunity presents itself. The mere existence of these naval platforms cannot be ignored by the enemy, who will be obliged to divert valuable resources to locate them, in the event that they leave their sidings. The German Navy used this strategy to capitalise its small number of surface ships during the First World War.[28]

Consequently, Argentine naval strategy in the 1980s was in a process of change and adaptation to her new combat platforms, which included the use of new missile systems, far better electronic software and updated operational procedures, all of which generated changes in doctrine and strategy. In short, the Argentine Navy´s modest surface forces had the ability to generate limited sea control strategies, but its rather small number of surface forces – and the inability to replace them – made such capability extremely difficult to maintain and very problematic if the adversary was a nuclear power, like Britain.

The Royal Navy and Argentine Naval Doctrine

By January 1982 the Argentine Navy had already invested a decade training its crews in the new weapon systems of British origin, among which were two brand new Type 42 guided missile destroyers which would operate with the new WG.13 Sea Lynx ASW high performance helicopter with its capacity to carry two Stingray torpedoes or four Sea Skua anti-ship missiles. This essential element of the ship produced by Westland had been specifically designed to operate from small ships in all-weather conditions, with easy maintenance. The official brochure of the British firm showed a photo of an Argentine Navy Lynx lifting a 300 lb. boat in mid-air. Because of these strong commercial ties, Britain had given Argentina a special place over other countries in the region, such as Chile and Brazil.

The Chilean Navy – another traditional client of the United Kingdom – since 1971 developed with the UK an important programme aimed at renewing part of its surface fleet. This included the construction and modernisation of several naval units, including the frigates *Lynch* and *Condell*, the submarines *O'Brien* and *Hyatt*, as well as the destroyers *Williams* and *Riveros*. However, as from 1975, Britain and Chile became more and more politically separated by human rights issues, thus the programme began to find all kinds of obstacles.

Quite the opposite occurred with the Argentine Navy. Argentine officers not only shared the same courses with their British peers but were also invited to all social events organised by the Royal Navy. There was a healthy camaraderie between the officers of both navies and, in general, a deep respect and admiration towards a friendly country, so there was no anger or hatred towards the future adversary.

In order to carry out limited sea control operations a task force was created around the carrier ARA *25 de Mayo*. This task force would need destroyers to provide point air defence. For this purpose, the Argentine Navy acquired two of the latest British Type 42 guided missile destroyers. The first destroyer, ARA *Hercules* (D-1) – sister ship of HMS *Sheffield* – was built at Vickers' shipyard in Barrow-in-Furness; the second one, ARA *Santisima Trinidad* (D-2) in AFNE shipyard in Buenos Aires under British supervision.

These naval units meant an important technological leap for the Navy. Its main weapon system, the GWS Mk-30 Sea Dart SAM with its twin launcher with a reserve of 22 missiles, was able to intercept aircraft flying at high altitude up to a maximum range of 65km; exceptionally – and in the absence of another type of weapon – it could also be used as an anti-ship missile. They displaced 4,250 tons at full load and could reach a maximum speed of 30 knots. Everything was on an economic scale in the Type 42s: one anchor, one galley, one workshop and one gangway. Its compact layout and its small-spaces design generally left little room to incorporate new weapon systems.

These ships, although the most modern in Latin America, had been designed in the late 1960s to provide the British fleet with area air defence. The Type 42 destroyer was intended to fulfil the same role, with similar systems on a smaller and more cost-effective hull.

As David Russell described:

> Radar systems on the destroyer included two Marconi Type-909 G/H-band tracking and target illuminating radars as part of its GWS 30 Sea Dart surface-to-air missile weapon control system and gun direction. The aiming and fire control functions for the Type 42 GMD's (guided missile destroyer's) Sea Dart missiles and 4.5-inch gun are provided by an ADAWS 4 action data automation weapon system.
>
> Integrated with the ... Marconi Type-965 A/B-band early warning air surveillance radar is the MEL-built SUSIE-III IFM system, with an EMI SARIE (selective automatic radar identification equipment) radar signal processor. Together this system is known as Britain's WLR-8 Abbey Hill. The SARIE system automatically analyzes [*sic*] and identifies radar pulses intercepted by the ship's sensors, and compares the intercepts with those contained in its dictionary (capacity: 476 radar types) within a fraction of a second.
>
> Also used ... was the Marconi Type-992Q E/R-band stabilized [*sic*] air/surface surveillance and target designation radar. Kelvin

Guided missile destroyer ARA *Hercules* (D-1) photographed in 1977 on her arrival to Puerto Belgrano Naval Base. Note that it has not yet been fitted with Exocet. (Argentine Navy)

> Hughes supplied the Type-1006 tactical radar for HDWS and helicopter control. Two eight barreled [*sic*] chaff launchers were fitted just below the aft radome.[29]

Its electronic equipment was mostly anti-aircraft with a limited anti-surface and naval gunfire fire support capability provided by a 4.5-inch Vickers Mk. 8 cannon of excellent precision and range, which did not satisfy the Argentine admirals. This later led to *Hercules* being fitted with four Exocet MM38 (42km range) missiles in order to give the ship a greater surface-to-surface capacity, something that distinguished her from her British sisters.

The fact that the first ship of the series – the *Sheffield* – was being built at the same time as the *Hercules* was a serious disadvantage considering that all its weapon systems had not been previously tested. This led, in practice, to share with the British the risks of any faulty results that usually occurred during the working up of a new ship. The *Hercules* was used by the British as a test laboratory, specially to overcome her faulty weapon systems and radars. Several of her parts were used in the *Sheffield* in order to deliver her in time to the Royal Navy.

The *Santisima Trinidad* had an even more problematic construction than her sister ship. Its keel was laid down at the AFNE shipyard in Rio Santiago on 11 October 1971, being launched on 9 November 1974. During the period of completion afloat, the ship suffered a terrorist attack on 22 August 1975 by the Montoneros Peronist movement. The ship suffered serious structural damage that caused her partial sinking in dock – its hull ended resting on the riverbed. Although she was later re-floated and subsequently transferred to a floating dock, her completion was greatly delayed. After conducting her sea trials and her weapons systems tuning in England she was finally commissioned in July 1981, just 10 months before the outbreak of the Falklands/Malvinas Conflict. Even then many technical problems persisted during her short operational life.

The *Sheffield* and her two Argentine sisters were the only units of the class initially fitted with the odd-looking '*Mickey Mouse* ears' type of funnel, which were in fact exhaust deflectors for the Rolls Royce Olympus gas turbines, necessary to guide the high-temperature exhaust side-wards and minimise damage to overhead aerials. As this provided a prominent target for the then new infrared homing missiles, all subsequent Olympus and Tyne uptakes were fitted with so-called *cheese graters* which mixed machinery space vent air with the engine exhaust to reduce infrared signatures.

Whoever advised the Argentine Navy to purchase the Type 42 destroyers was wrong. The combat experience collected later in the Falklands/Malvinas conflict showed that the 'cheap' Type 42 destroyers were a false economy for those who employed them, because of their much higher degree of vulnerability, as demonstrated by the sinking of two Royal Navy ships of these class. Their sensors and radars were unreliable most of the time, and thus inadequate for the first war of the missile age.

The capacity of warships to take damage without unduly impairing their capacity to perform their tasks has often proved crucial. During the Falklands/Malvinas campaign the British expensively relearned the dangers of cutting costs (specially in fire retardation) when fitting out their ships. A sense of being excessively vulnerable to damage or loss might, more generally, lead to a decline in readiness to take risks that often proved to be an essential component of successful tactics.[30]

The Falklands/Malvinas Conflict and Naval Strategy

The gunboat diplomacy that preceded the South Atlantic campaign of 1982 showed both sides using their naval forces as the means to express their national interests in the Falklands/Malvinas dispute. Argentina had frequently used the Navy to indicate its distaste for the existing situation, as occurred on 4 February 1976 when the destroyer ARA *Almirante Storni* (Commander Ramón Arosa) made intimidating fire on the bow of the British research vessel RRS *Shackleton* which was sailing in Argentine territorial waters, and despite being ordered to stop, refused to be inspected. This incident culminated in the rupture of diplomatic relations between the two countries and although the Argentine government made complaints regarding the reckless conduct observed by the British captain, the latter claimed in his defence to be in international waters – 78 miles from Port Stanley – and carrying explosives on board, an excuse that was accepted by the British Court of Admiralty.

For their part, the British maintained for years the polar ship HMS *Endurance* and a small garrison of Royal Marines on the islands to symbolise the support of the Crown and deter greater attempts by Argentina. In light of what happened in 1982 this level of strength proved to be too low to achieve its goal. The deterrence failed again when in 1977 a mini task force was secretly dispatched to the Falklands/Malvinas area – a nuclear attack submarine with the support of some surface ships, HMS *Alacrity* (F-174), and HMS *Phoebe* (F-42), of whose presence the Argentine´s never found out – to reinforce the British negotiating position. This 'contingent

The ceremony of change of command on board ARA *Salta* during 1979. (Photo by Roberto Salinas)

One of the US-manufactured Amtracs that landed in the Falklands/Malvinas on 2 April, now on display in a Museum in the main base of the Marine Corps at Baterias, near the small town of Punta Alta, in the province of Buenos Aires. (Author's collection)

positioning'[31] had no effect because Argentina was not militarily deterred, nor was it aware of the potential cost of landing on the islands. Thus, the attack on a British vessel and other additional measures – the installation of a scientific base on Thule Island, South Sandwich – did not find any known British response, outside the return to the negotiating table.

The failure of British deterrence during the Malvinas crisis of 1982 was largely due to the erroneous assumptions made by both parties regarding the intentions and capabilities of the other. The United Kingdom underestimated the Argentine intentions of landing on the islands; Argentina, in turn, underestimated Britain's capacity to react to recover them before disembarking in East Falkland and South Georgia and from there she continued to underestimate it – especially when launching a military adventure without any strategic ally and without having solved the prevailing border dispute with Chile, in order to avoid a possible second front. The result was a war that nobody wanted.

In March 1982, the Junta used the scrap metal incident in South Georgia as an excuse to escalate the dispute with Britain and launch the Malvinas operation. The Junta sabotaged the only concrete gesture of British aggression that had materialised until that moment, by deploying two corvettes between South Georgia and the Falkland/Malvinas Islands. The presence of these ships naturally discouraged the British government from trying to expel Argentine personnel from Leith by force, something that from the diplomatic point of view was essential to sustain the Argentine position before the international community. As Mrs Thatcher commented on that occasion: 'We knew that if we took them out by force they would threaten us; the *Endurance* would have been stopped and there were ships to do it'.[32]

Encouraged by this success, the Argentine government began phase two of its plan that could be framed in what James Cable calls 'the application of defining force',[33] that is, a determined attempt to cut the path in the normal process of diplomacy, presenting the adversary something close to the *fait accompli* when giving the green light for Operation Azul.

The question is thus: why Operation Azul/Rosario failed as an act of naval compulsion force to end the dispute? Undoubtedly because the British considered such result as unacceptable and essentially felt that they had the diplomatic and military means that gave them reasonable possibilities to do something about it and reach a different solution to the problem. The subsequent dispatch of the Royal Navy's Task Force – Operation Corporate – also failed to persuade the Argentines to leave the islands peacefully, nor did it convince them to reach a diplomatic solution acceptable to the British. There seem to be two reasons for this.

First, the military Junta continued to overestimate its own military power in relation to Britain, putting too much faith in the defence of the islands by the Argentine Army – which had no experience in war, and as a result had taken static defensive positions – in the attack capabilities of its Air Force, and in the strategic effectiveness of its small arsenal of Exocets. This hypothesis, although reasonable – given the inexperience in war of the Argentine armed forces – was unrealistic and naïve considering that they were challenging a major world power like Great Britain, a cornerstone of NATO. Ironically, the Royal Navy was an adversary that was well known to the Argentine Navy, which placed her in a better position to assess the risks. However, other actors also shared the Argentine point of view, including some key US military advisers.

Second, if the main objective of the Royal Navy's Task Force was to persuade the Argentines to leave peacefully – and this debate remains open – the Argentines could well have misunderstood the British motivations and instead concluded from the response given by the United Kingdom – through its decline to explore ways of transferring sovereignty diplomatically, the symbolic capture of South Georgia, and the declaration and implementation of the different exclusion zones – that, strictly speaking, the hostilities had begun and now it was too late – in political terms – to withdraw from the islands with honour. If this was indeed the case and if the British thought to dispatch the task force in terms of *non-lethal compulsion*, then it had precisely the opposite effect to that desired, by triggering a general Argentine mobilisation that it was intended to avoid – and

The landing ship ARA *Cabo San Antonio* in an old photo probably taken in Puerto Madryn. (Argentine Navy Photo)

which graphically illustrates – the dangers and deficiencies of using a naval force in this way.

From this perspective, the use of maritime forces – naval compulsion – to directly pursue specific political objectives is clearly a difficult and imprecise art. The opponent may misunderstand the motivation behind the act of force and may react unexpectedly.

Another problem for the British was the enormous distance that separated them from the disputed area and their adversaries. The transit time it would take the fleet to reach it – two weeks – placed them in the difficult position of deciding the answer before knowing the challenge and the magnitude of the opposition they faced.

This brief analysis of how both sides sought to use their naval forces as instruments of diplomacy allows us to conclude that it was an immensely complex process, in which many things could go wrong, and almost all of them did. Naval diplomacy of this kind is a difficult and dangerous matter, where errors of judgment and perception abound.

However, the essential justification for this type of naval manoeuvring is that they can collaborate in decompressing a situation of diplomatic tension in order to avoid a major conflict. In the case of the Falklands/Malvinas crisis, this did not happen. The British failed to dissuade; Argentina failed to redefine the situation according to its own interests. For these reasons the crisis began to slide into war.

But it would be a one-of-a-kind war. It was not – as Michael Howard pointed out – a *total war* between two adversaries determined to completely defeat the other, without measuring human or material losses. On the contrary it was a limited war, with limited means in pursuit of limited objectives. It was a conflict that confirmed with total clarity the advantages of sea power to lead limited wars, as enunciated by maritime strategists such as Sir Julian Corbett. Both belligerents found themselves operating in a perpetual half-light, where the political logic of the events was at least as important as the military.[34]

The contribution of naval power in the final outcome of the Falklands/Malvinas campaign was widely demonstrated. The Falklands/Malvinas War served to observe, for example, the importance of national resources and styles of government in determining the character of maritime power, and its influence on the way it is used in war. Analysts seem to have agreed that after a hesitant start, the British established a war machine that generally worked excellently. This contrasted totally with the situation in Buenos Aires, where the campaign situation was seriously compromised by the chaotic state of the government and the sharp inter-service rivalry, which reflected a country approaching its political and economic collapse. In particular, the preponderant role of Admiral Jorge Anaya – head of the Argentine Navy – demonstrated the risks, both military and political, of a flag officer

The author beside a Douglas A-4Q Skyhawk (3-A-302) now on display in the Naval Aviation Museum at Espora Naval Station, near Bahia Blanca. (author's private collection)

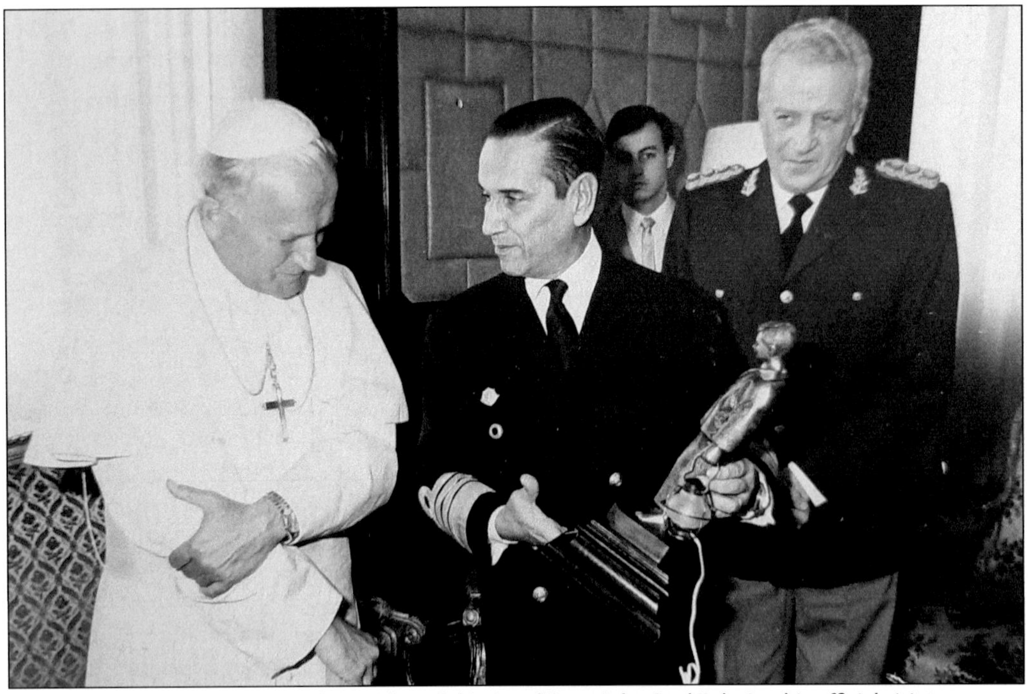

Admiral Jorge Anaya with President Galtieri and Pope John Paul II during his official visit to Argentina (11 June 1982) at the end of the Falklands/Malvinas War. (Photo by Guillermo Anaya)

who saw himself as a politician, rather than the mere instrument of a given policy.

For the British, the main difficulty lay in the conduct of an intense – and possibly prolonged – conflict in an extremely inhospitable area, far removed from British home bases. In this respect Ascension Island – located 4,600nm from the UK – proved invaluable to reduce the enormous logistical challenge to more manageable proportions. That small volcanic island became the forward operating base for the Royal Navy, a true training centre for troops, and an anchorage where ships could replenish essential materials, mail and men. Wideawake Airfield lived up to its name and – for a while – became the busiest airport in the world. Ascension was also valuable as a communications centre, manoeuvring area and military airfield from where air defence aircraft, powerful scouts and Vulcan bombers operated. After the conflict, the Commander-in-Chief of the British fleet, Admiral Sir John Fieldhouse, in a letter to the administrator of the island said: 'Ascension was crucial to the success of the operation.' Aware of its strategic importance – halfway to the theatre of operations – the British always feared an Argentine coup de main, which would have substantially dismantled their war effort.[35]

Maritime geography, in a more general sense, also helped determine the nature of the conflict. If the islands had been 150 miles closer or further from Argentina´s mainland, the nature of the conflict would have been totally different. The development of operations also had a rather critical dependence on weather. Despite all the equipment of modern technology, the commanders of surface units at sea and the jet pilots on land, scrutinised the sky every morning with the same anxiety with which their predecessors always did.

The permanent contribution of a nation's merchant navy to its naval power was also absolutely demonstrated. On the Argentine side it was merchant ships such as the ELMA *Rio de la Plata* (Captain Carlos Benchetrit) who gave *early warning* of the existence of a powerful enemy naval force concentrated on Ascension Island, sending the first signals to the Argentine Naval HQ in Buenos Aires about the strength of the enemy naval forces. These ships were also responsible for circumventing the British blockade around the islands – at the risk of being attacked by their own aircraft – as in the cases of, for example, *Narwal* and *Isla de los Estados*. Following the implementation by Great Britain of the Total Maritime Exclusion Zones, an airlift was carried out to replace these ships.

On the British side the effort of the merchant navy was even greater. Three large ocean liners, 15 tankers, eight roll-on-roll-off general cargo ships, a container ship, a cable-laying vessel, five fishing vessels, four mixed cargo and passenger ships, six general cargo ships, several tugboats and support ships were requisitioned and forced to serve in a great variety of indispensable functions. Many of these ships had to be adapted to be used in wartime with helicopter platforms, refuelling equipment at sea and so on. The fact that so many merchant ships were rapidly converted and sent to the front line – practically without prior notice – has been a considerable tribute to the permanent versatility of the shipyards and naval repair shops in the United Kingdom. Some 330 officers and 1,170 merchant ship crews set sail with the ships, which were often in high-risk situations.

The Royal Navy's Task Force was also supported by 22 Royal Fleet Auxiliaries – mostly large tankers – refuelling ships and logistic landing vessels, although for them it was a more familiar function. After the conflict was over, Jim Slater – the leader of the National Union of Seamen – summed up the situation with the following words: 'Without the support provided by the Merchant Navy, the Royal Navy would have stayed in port.'[36]

Argentina´s national merchant navy (ELMA) was dismantled years after the war. As for the local shipyards, once a source of a reliable naval industry, are now practically paralysed. That strategic industry was allowed to disperse, and was practically abandoned by the state; therefore, it will not be available in times of national emergency.

In conclusion, the Falklands/Malvinas War demonstrated that the traditional factors of naval power remained as decisive for success in wartime as when Mahan and others struggled to identify them. The technological, political and economic changes produced since then do not seem to have substantially reduced the value of these premises, at least in this kind of war.

The Junta´s Naïve Strategy

The new Argentinian military Junta was sworn into office on 18 December 1981. Brigadier General Lami Dozo of the Air Force had been promoted into the body on 1 December; Admiral Anaya had headed the navy since 11 September; and General Galtieri had been in charge of the Army since March.

When the military became involved in politics, and begun running the country in March 1976, each service had precisely 33.3 percent of everything: power, responsibility, military budget,

Table 1: Argentine Merchant Ships operating in logistics role during the Falklands/ Malvinas War, 1982

Ship's name	Displacement	Ship-owner	Captain	Fate
Rio Cancel	10,070 tons	ELMA	Trivelin, J.	
Rio Carcaraña	10,200 tons	ELMA	Dell Elicine, E.	Sunk
Formosa	20,704 tons	ELMA	Gregorio, J.	Attacked by FAA A-4Bs
Cordoba	10,200 tons	ELMA	Malvich, J.	
Bahia Buen Suceso	5,000 tons	NAVAL TRANS	Niella, Osvaldo	Sunk
Isla de Los Estados	3,900 tons	NAVAL TRANS	Panigadi, Tulio	Sunk
Mar del Norte	4,529 tons	LA NAVIERA	Juarez, Pedro	

Table 2: Smaller Argentine vessels and Fishing Trawlers operating in Intelligence-Gathering Role during the Falklands/Malvinas War, 1982

Ship's name	Displacement	Ship-owner	Captain	Fate
Tierra del Fuego II	25,000 tons	ELMA	Curria, Hector	
Rio de La Plata	12,000 tons	ELMA	Benchetrit, C	
Maria Alejandra	669 tons	AGENTE MARITIMO AMALFITANO	Quagliarella, Luis	
Narwal	1,400 tons	COMPAÑIA SUDAMERICANA DE PESCA	Fabiano, Nestor	Sunk
Constanza	600 tons	PESQUERA ARPEMAR	Dabos, Roberto	

had created a situation where senior officers felt free to pass judgment, not only on their professional field, but on politics in general.[38]

This is an important element for the understanding of how the decision to retake the Falkland/Malvinas Islands was made.

Argentina´s conspiracy theorists – always present within the military – started to see the problem of the Falklands/Malvinas as joined with British claims in Antarctica and as part of the Anglo-Chilean collusion in the Beagle Channel. Under the new military government of 1976-1979, problems with Chile had escalated into a border clash that occurred between 1977-1978. A last-minute offer by the Vatican to mediate was accepted by both parties, and war was prevented. The Vatican decision became known in December 1980. By it, the Pope awarded the islands in the Beagle Channel to Chile. This had a major impact in Argentina´s balance of power considerations in the Southern Cone of South America.[39]

The international context in Gamba´s expert opinion was as follows:

> Until 1980, negotiations with Britain over the South Atlantic territories had not been conditioned by time. Nevertheless, with the Beagle Channel dispute and the assignment of those territories to Chile, military strategists in Argentina felt that their Antarctic claims and the Argentinian presence in the sub-Antarctic needed to be reinforced by a final negotiation with the United Kingdom over the Falkland/Malvinas Islands. The logic behind this implied that if Argentina was definitely going to lose the islands within the Beagle Channel, then that loss of ground would be balanced by a formal and definitive negotiation with the United Kingdom over the Falkland/Malvinas Islands. If we understand that the greatest fear in Argentina was a future Anglo-Chilean collusion in the sub-Antarctic, then it is easy for us to comprehend the necessity in Buenos Aires for Great Britain to be seen as complying to a definitive negotiation on the sovereignty issue so that there would be no doubt in the area relating to Argentina´s claims. This does not mean that a transfer of sovereignty was necessarily immediate; it merely states that the perception of a progressive and final negotiation was vital for balance of power considerations in the area regarding Argentina.[40] The years 1978 and 1979 had marked an increasingly hard line toward Chile, but at the same time had shown a new relaxation of the Anglo-Argentinian dispute over the Falkland/Malvinas Islands. The new Junta was not prepared to let this happen, and had already begun to plan a military intervention – as we have seen in chapter 1 – by

ministries and so forth. No joint or unified command existed, and no inter-force communication or training, except at the very top: the military Junta.

Argentine scholar, Virginia Gamba, writing about the Falklands/ Malvinas War points out:

> For decades, the old-fashioned Argentine military institutions had undermined the power of both the Ministry of Defence and the Joint Chiefs of Staff; thus, these organizations [*sic*] were mere buildings where senior officers with no future in the hierarchy spent their time before early retirement. The armed forces managed military affairs in a feudal spirit, each directing strategy and politics from their respective buildings in Buenos Aires: Cóndor (HQ of the Air Force), Libertad (HQ of the Navy) and Libertador (HQ of the Army).[37]

The aforementioned system enabled Admiral Anaya and the Junta to decide on their own how to handle Anglo-Argentine relations and assess the regional balance of power and territorial considerations in the region as they saw fit, without resorting to any other government departments or institution. Three decision centres had been set up, each one hundreds of miles apart. National strategy was made in Buenos Aires, military strategy in Puerto Belgrano, and operational strategy in Port Stanley.

Gamba confirms this when writing in regard to the Junta´s inner proceedings:

> Argentina had developed over the past 50 years into a typical "praetorian society", where institutions were not strong and the heavy bureaucracy immobilised everything; people cared more about "personality" than about institutions. The same was true of the military. The system was deficient, and this showed in its hour of need. The politicisation of the military, plus the "praetorianism"

ordering Vice Admiral Lombardo to prepare to invade the islands on 15 December 1981. The question was when to do so.

The landing of Davidoff's men in Leith Harbour in the early hours of 19 March 1982 by the transport ship ARA *Bahia Buen Suceso* would start the South Georgia crisis, which in turn would trigger the Falklands/Malvinas War.

Throughout the difficult hours of the crisis that led to the recovery of the Falkland/Malvinas Islands, many instances were noted in which the governor and pressure groups – interested in magnifying the size of the incidents – managed to influence the Foreign Office, ruining any possibility of negotiation.[41]

An offer by the Argentine Foreign Minister – made on 25 March 1982 – was rejected by the British. In this offer – which appears in paragraph 198 of the Franks Report – the Argentine Foreign Minister indicated Argentina's goodwill for Davidoff's workers to walk to Grytviken and complete the necessary landing formalities by having their white cards stamped at Grytviken. It is interesting to note that the British ambassador in Buenos Aires recommended this course of action to London, in view of the risk of military confrontation. However, it would be Governor Hunt who put an obstacle in the way of peaceful settlement of the dispute by this method, since he advised London that the white card regime did not apply in this case because South Georgia was a dependency of the Falkland/Malvinas Islands not included in the 1971 Communications Agreement signed by both countries, and that if the Ministry of Foreign Affairs had issued white cards, this indicated its involvement in Mr. Davidoff's plans. However, he agreed on stamping the Argentine passports rather than their white cards. This course of action would recognise the Argentineans as foreigners, in a territory that both parties considered their own.[42] This was too much for the Junta to tolerate; they deliberately left aside other diplomatic solutions – for example, extract the workers from the island by an Argentine vessel or permit the British to evict them by force – and manipulated the incident to use it as an excuse to invade the islands.

Up to then no Argentine government had taken such an action for the past 100 years. By doing so they would be breaking a long and cherished diplomatic tradition in the country – that of not solving foreign policy problems by force. The British knew that a military intervention by Argentina was atypical in the decision-making process apparatus in the country, and because of that, Argentina was considered a passive actor in the dispute, not a potential aggressor.[43] They would change that perception backed by the ill advice given by their senior diplomatic advisers, convinced that Britain would not and could not react militarily.

Another major problem for Argentina was the lack of experience in this sort of action. The latest military activity in the country had consisted of fighting a sub-limited war against rural and urban guerrillas. Even this experience had been gained on the spot rather than as a result of planning or previous study. Moreover, the restructuring of military institutions over the past 15 years had been centred on guerrilla warfare and for these objectives. A conventional war had not been considered, and the probability of ever fighting with a foreign nation had been neglected for many decades. The country also did not have the capabilities to cope with more than one kind of warfare at any given time. Contingency planning for sub-limited war, most probable in Argentina, had conditioned the military against other types of conflict.[44]

All the Argentine planners had in January 1982 was a conflict hypothesis with Britain, even though plans for this hypothesis had not been completed nor had a set date. In spite of this, the military Junta decided to embark on an April military intervention during the week in which all army conscripts were licensed – a normal yearly procedure – the air force lacked replacement parts and new aircraft, the navy's Super Etendard jets had not arrived from France – except for a limited number – and the Exocet missiles had not only not arrived in full – only five had been delivered – but also had not been modified to act in combination with the Etendards. In addition, the few existing Etendards had not been adapted to be able to operate from the Argentine aircraft carrier.[45]

This lack of elementary preparations confirm that Admiral Anaya made this bold move without the knowledge of the Navy's officer corps, causing a cultural fracture within the service, probably because he was convinced that the crisis would not end in an open conventional war with Great Britain.

The Junta had convinced itself that an intervention with a limited scope would eventually force Britain to negotiate. Argentina's policy of damage limitation during the original 2 April 1982 intervention had been motivated by the desire to (a) advance slowly the use of force – starting the necessary escalation at the lowest level of bloodshed possible – (b) maintain its political objective – forcing Britain to negotiate – and (c) offset its self-perception of lack of credibility in the international arena.[46]

Limited bloodshed, an immediate repatriation of prisoners, and respect/liberty for the inhabitants of the islands, plus a rapid withdrawal of troops from them were designed to press the point home regarding Argentina's limited objectives. The British government did not get the message and prepared to wage war with everything they had, including US military assistance.

When at the last moment the Navy was told of Operation Azul/Rosario, it prepared to engage the enemy with its flags and institutional preferences flying proudly, even though it knew that it would be something like the Charge of the Light Brigade.

3
CULTURE AND OPERATIONS IN THE SOUTH ATLANTIC

> There are profound differences between a battle where both sides wish for a full trial of strength and skill, and a battle where one side has no intention of fighting to a finish, and seeks only to retire without disadvantage or dishonour from an unequal and undesired combat. The problems before the Commanders, the conditions of the conflict itself, are widely different in a fleeting encounter – no matter how large its scale – from those of a main trial of strength. In an encounter between forces obviously unequal, the object of the weaker is to escape, and that of the stronger to catch and destroy them.[1]

With these words Winston Churchill described the preliminaries of the Battle of Jutland, but those same words could have been used for the battle at sea in the Falklands/Malvinas conflict. Unlike Jutland, during the Falklands/Malvinas War there was no contact between the surface forces of both sides; however, this passage resembles in many ways the behaviour of both naval contenders in the South Atlantic conflict. The old axiom that *maritime power is to win and keep control of the sea for one´s own use, and to deny such control to one´s adversaries* was a very old belief that was present in the Falklands/Malvinas conflict, but even in the light of historical experience, neither control nor its denial can reasonably be expected to prove complete, permanent or universal. It has often happened that control has remained in dispute.[2]

Control of the sea depends on the resources available, the nature of the conflict and the priority attaching to the particular uses of the sea which is intended either to protect or to deny. It is the first of these factors that has received most attention, and traditional theory assumed that sea control and ultimate victory could be expected to reward the stronger navy. It is no secret that the Argentine Navy had a high regard for the Royal Navy – probably because of the legacy of Britain´s Great Power status. In military, naval and economic terms Britain was among the small group of European states which were clearly stronger than all the rest. England still retained the ability to wage war – on a modest scale, wherever necessary – against any state.

In that context Rear Admiral Gualter Allara – the man who commanded the only Argentine Carrier Task Force in 1982 – said after the war ended that 'it was suicidal to place the fleet between Ascension and the Falkland/Malvinas Islands, it would mean to lose the fleet without any reason, especially knowing that the enemy had permanent information about the position of our ships'.[3] If there was one thing of Argentine naval thinking prior to the outbreak of war, it was the tendency to credit the Royal Navy with far greater audacity and willingness to take risks against odds than either the Argentine themselves would have shown or than the British in fact did show when the test came.

Carrier ARA *25 de Mayo* (Argentine hull number V-2; Colossus-class; ex-HMS *Venerable*, ex-HNLMS *Karel Doorman*; displacement 19,900 tonnes) during exercises in the South Atlantic in 1980. (Argentine Navy)

Eventually, the striking power of the air-launched missiles and the hunter-killer nuclear attack submarines would be the dominant factors in the war at sea. This distinctive approach to warfare in the cold waters of the South Atlantic Ocean reveals an enormous amount about the significance of institutional culture in the Argentine Navy.

According to Julian Corbett, maritime strategy defines 'what part the fleet must play in relation to the action of land forces' and its paramount concern is to 'determine the mutual relations of the army and navy in a plan of war'.[4] These inter-service relations did not exist within the Argentine armed forces in 1982.

However, the Argentine Navy followed Corbett´s principles in regard to the *Methods of Defensive Fleet Operations*, in what he called a *fleet-in-being approach*, which dictated the following: 'At sea the main conception is avoiding decisive action by strategical [*sic*] or tactical activity, so as to keep our fleet-in-being, till the situation develops in our favour. The idea was to dispute the control by harassing operations, to exercise control … in spite of his [the enemy´s] superiority by continually occupying his attention.'[5] This approach is of particular value for a fleet that knows itself inferior to its adversary – in number or quality – and cannot realistically hope to gain or contest command of the sea by the normal method.

In some ways there is an analogy between the fleet-in-being approach and the principles of guerrilla warfare. Even Mahan thought an active fleet-in-being strategy could yield considerably more useful results than either accepting battle with a superior enemy and losing or, on the one hand, letting the fleet rot at anchor.

This defensive strategy was reinforced by the fact that both contenders at the time operated identical weapons systems such as Sea King and Sea Lynx helicopters, Exocet missiles and Type 42 destroyers. The British even had to paint a black line down the stack and hull of their own Type 42 destroyers to avert any confusion – if they met at sea – with the Argentine ships of the same class.

Both nations were conscious that this would be the first major naval engagement since the end of the Second World War in the Pacific: the Argentine Navy had trained for years to confront Chile or Brazil, not an extra-regional enemy like the United Kingdom, none other than the third naval power in the world. This determined the Argentine Navy to shift its operational strategy as the enemy´s intentions unfolded in the theatre of operations.

The symbolism of the capital surface ship was mirrored in the role of the aircraft carrier ARA *25 de Mayo* and the light cruiser ARA *General Belgrano*, which constituted the core of the Argentine fleet, and whose intervention dominated offensive operations during the first days of the conflict. This cultural characteristic of the naval service confirms that in the Argentine Navy of the 1980s the capital ships still dominated naval thinking. Aircraft and torpedoes were important but were viewed as secondary weapons.

In this context the Argentine fleet operations can be divided into two very distinct stages:

1) Initial manoeuvres (28 March – 2 May): After concluding Operation Azul/Rosario successfully, the Argentine Navy´s surface fleet was deployed in successive Task Groups in view to neutralise enemy surface forces or to engage British naval units that could be tied up by an amphibious landing with the object of preventing the British from consolidating a beachhead in the islands; and
2) War of attrition (2 May – 14 June): After the sinking of the light cruiser ARA *General Belgrano* the Navy decided to employ the fleet-in-being concept, conscious of the necessity to retain a reserve naval capacity in case of a possible post-war Chilean aggression. The Argentine Navy´s top brass made up its mind not to compromise its surface forces in a decisive battle with the Royal Navy opting instead for a war of attrition.[6]

A rare view from the bow of the light cruiser ARA *General Belgrano* (Argentine hull number C-4; ex-USS *Phoenix*, CL-46; displacement 13,500 tonnes). Note its main armament of triple 6-inch guns visible here on two of the three forward turrets. (Author's private collection)

Guided missile destroyer ARA *Hercules* (Argentine hull number D-1), during her SAT trials in Barrow-in-Furness, UK, note the shipyard number 28 allotted to the ship still painted on her hull. (Argentine Navy Photo)

In addition, the Navy was facing another important challenge: to work in conjunction with the other two armed forces. This – as it was to be expected – generated multiple frictions and misunderstandings. That such disputes existed should not surprise anyone. Three different services were trying to carry out an unprecedented

Carrier ARA *25 de Mayo* sailing somewhere in the South Atlantic Ocean during 1980. (Argentine Navy)

operation that none of the three had even remotely anticipated before the war. Achieving success would require an overwhelming degree of inter-service coordination and cooperation.

The brief duration of the conflict – 74 days – did not prevent joint operations at the tactical and operational levels; unfortunately, this did not happen at the more significant strategic level. In almost all instances, it was the initiative of the tactical commanders who left aside the institutional culture of each service to confront a common enemy.

The tragic sinking of the cruiser ARA *General Belgrano* while sailing to a pre-arranged waiting area – outside the Total Exclusion Zone – was the baptism of fire of the Argentine fleet, a new and traumatic experience for the Navy. At the same time, it confirmed the worst fears of the Naval High Command regarding the presence in the operational theatre of enemy nuclear attack submarines, whose number and location were unknown. From that moment on, the surface fleet played a subordinate role with respect to the air and land dimension of the conflict, as we shall see later.

The lack of a single in-theatre commander to conduct operations, that is, an overall Commander-in-Chief that could coordinate efforts and combat actions against the enemy, forced the tactical level to improvise on-the-job solutions, trying to obtain the best possible results with the available means. Finally, the underlying conviction that Britain would not react militarily due to the complexity of such an operation and the logistical problems involved, and that – even in the case of trying – the United States would oppose a military escalation in the continent, meant that the military Junta handed over the initiative to the enemy. It was not realised that a more realistic assessment of the passive reaction attributed to the United Kingdom, without any serious argument, would have made the achievement of the strategic objective unlikely and disproportionate in view of the previsions adopted. This was what ultimately happened, and the *occupy-to-negotiate strategy* had to be shifted into *reinforce-to-deter* the United Kingdom to recover the islands by force in order to negotiate.

The light cruiser ARA *General Belgrano* during manoeuvres in 1978. (Argentine Navy)

Cruiser *General Belgrano* in her berth at Puerto Belgrano Naval Base in 1980. (Photo by author)

naval doctrine in case of war to be followed by the officer corps. With few exceptions, its doctrine, training and preparation for fighting enemy ships in missile combat had to be based on the experiences of other navies. On this aspect, Vice Admiral Juan Lombardo reflected after the conflict was over: 'Argentina had had a very long period of external peace until 1982: none of us, civilians or militaries, had any experience of war, of the intense trauma that war is … In all human activity, theoretical knowledge is important, but practical experience is irreplaceable.'[9]

It is well documented that the relationship between technology and naval strategy has been characterised by revolutionary developments that enhanced naval capabilities and performance of new technology. The boundaries of operational naval strategy were arguably more complex than previously experienced in history due to technological advance. Naval warfare has always been a high-technology environment; however, the introduction of computer automated systems and missiles has created more pressure on the human element to implement the traditional principles involved in naval strategy.

One of the most significant consequences of the effect of modern technology on the parameters of naval strategy and tactics has been the reduction in reaction times to incoming threats.[10] One such threat – which had never before been tested in real combat conditions – was the all-weather Exocet AM39 missile, a *fire-and-forget* weapon which had complete autonomous guidance, controlled in the first part of its flight by inertial navigation, then by active radar homing in the terminal phase.[11] Argentina possessed a very limited amount of these missiles, but they were a winning card that could cause real havoc among the enemy fleet; that´s why the Navy was obliged to make each missile count. In just 15 days the system was made operational by Argentine engineers and local technicians. However, it depended ultimately on the Etendard pilots to launch each one of them in the proper way at minimal range in order not to miss the target. In the end it was a team effort that paid

The Technological Dimension

Alastair Finlan noted correctly that 'naval strategy is composed of several interrelated factors, notably, institutional beliefs about how to fight, experience in war, technology and the enemy'.[7] In the case of the Argentine Navy of 1982, only one of the four factors had remained relatively constant within the ever-shifting synthesis: *institutional beliefs*.

Institutional beliefs about naval strategy vary between navies of different states: this accounts for why the Argentine Navy pointed out from the outset of the South Atlantic conflict the limited use of surface forces, except in the case of locating profitable targets or a favourable opportunity.[8] It was no secret that the Argentine Navy did not have any combat experience on which to draw, or a tested

The Super Etendard (3-A-205) fighter-bomber fitted with an AM39 Exocet to its wing. Here seen with the group of naval aviators that flew it in combat missions during the war. (Photo by Julio Barraza)

off. David Hart Dyke recalls of the Exocet that hit *Sheffield* on 4 May 1982:

> … an Exocet travelling at hundreds of miles an hour and skimming the sea´s surface below the reach of *Sheffield*´s radar coverage – and doing so at precisely the same time as the ship´s detection equipment, through a technical limitation, failed to pick up the fleeting radar transmissions from either the aircraft or the missile itself – was bound to get through. And it would only have needed a momentary lapse in concentration on the part of one of the warfare team in the operations room to miss a vital piece of information – that tiny, flickering radar echo – which would have triggered the alarm. Such is the nature of warfare in the missile age.[12]

As described above, computers and missiles are still dependent on individuals to utilise them effectively; thus, the degree of readiness of a warship varies from the training of the crew and the reliability of one weapon system to another, as it was shown by the unexpected sinking of HMS *Sheffield* and other ships. This aspect had a tremendous impact in both navies' operational strategy.

The Type 42s, for example, were very unreliable combat platforms because their electronics and sensors were outdated for this kind of high-tech war. The former captain of HMS *Coventry* – a Type 42 destroyer (hull number D118) – remembered:

> …the type [*sic*] 42s were demanding ships, requiring a very high degree of skill to keep all their systems functioning – something you might not always be able to guarantee, especially on prolonged operations. There always seemed to be times when one ship or another had defective radar or weapon, and this inevitably put a considerable strain on the others.[13]

Admiral Sandy Woodward himself seems to agree with this point of view. Recalling his time in HMS *Sheffield*, he said:

> Type 42s cost close to 200 million pounds to build. How come whenever they went out in a big sea for a period of several hours their main weapons systems crashed immediately afterwards, because water is rushing in where it plainly ought not to be? I knew from my own time in *Sheffield* that the 42s were not as fast as they should be, that they were unreasonably slow in a short swell, with the bows slamming into the waves rather than splitting them to each side cleanly…[14]

The Argentine Navy, as already mentioned, had two warships of this class and their crews had been trained in the United Kingdom, so they were in a unique position to exploit their strengths and weaknesses. From very early on the Argentine crews knew of the multiple deficiencies of the Type 42s and tried very hard to solve them but came rapidly to the conclusion that in case of war the ships would have lots of liabilities.

The Royal Navy – trained to act against an adversary with completely different doctrine and equipment – found itself unexpectedly confronted against a navy that used its same doctrine and even its own units and equipment. Additionally, the need to operate within the radius of action of Argentine strike aircraft against an opponent who knew the defences of the Royal Navy, added to the lack of airborne early warning, eventually led to the sinking of six ships and various degrees of damage to some 25 others. This parity in weapon systems was reflected in a remark made by Captain Jeremy Black, the CO of HMS *Invincible* just before the outbreak of war: 'Exocet vs. Exocet, Hum! That´s not nice!'[15]

The Strategy of David Against Goliath

The balance between the two fleets – including naval aviation forces – was very dynamic, and the tendency was decidedly in favour of

A Super Etendard seen during landing, with its arrestor hook down. Serial number 3-A-209 identifies this aircraft as one of those embargoed during the war of 1982: while delivered to Argentina only after the conflict, its overall appearance is the same as that of the five examples that flew combat operations in May 1982. (Argentine Navy)

Argentina. It is appropriate to recall that the conflict took place shortly after a marked change in the priorities of British defence policy, which particularly affected their surface fleet. The irony that a maritime effort of such magnitude was required shortly after this revision was quickly signalled by the press, highlighting that the Task Force was getting ready in soon to be closed arsenals, which would be headed by two ASW aircraft carriers – HMS *Hermes* and HMS *Invincible* – to be eliminated prematurely, and that it was manned by sailors, hundreds of whom kept their discharge papers in their pockets. At the same time, the Argentine Navy was engaged in a significant programme of renewal of its warships and naval aviation platforms. Recent acquisitions, although still in the construction stage, included four MEKO 360 class frigates built in Germany, along with two TR-1700-class submarines, six MEKO 140 corvettes, plus 14 Super Etendard aircraft and more Exocet AM39 missiles.

Royal Marines surrender at Government House on 2 April 1982. Here escorted by men of the Buzo Tactico special forces team. (Photo by Rafael Wollmann)

Rear Admiral Carlos Büsser, General Garcia, and Rear Admiral Gualter Allara talk after the takeover of the Falkland/Malvinas Islands. (Argentine Navy)

That the ruling Junta did not wait for some time until the strategic balance was decidedly in their favour is inexplicable and suggests that – like other previous governments – it misread the direction the world was heading in, and what role Argentina had in it. They clearly had an idealised vision about the importance of the country. They were thus unable to assume its poor strategic significance in the eyes of the United States and her ally – the United Kingdom – and to deploy a serious, professional and efficient diplomacy that would have allowed them to read the intentions of their future adversary in advance.

Thus, we may conclude that the decision of the Junta to bring forward the date of execution of Operation Azul/Rosario was misguided, and the only thing it caused was the escalation of the conflict to a point of no return, without completing full-scale planning and the necessary concurrent provisions, placing their own armed forces in an extremely vulnerable position, for which they were not prepared.

Operation Azul/Rosario

The way in which the Argentine Navy tackled the occupation of the Falkland/Malvinas Islands reflects this conclusion when choosing an amphibious operation that – although successful – showed an overwhelming deployment of means and men on a scale clearly superior to that necessary to face such a tiny opponent.[16]

When Rear Admiral Carlos Büsser – Commander of the Amphibious Assault Force – was consulted, after the conflict was over, if the number of men who had intervened in the operation were not too many for the 76 Royal Marines in charge of defending the islands, he said: 'Not at all, I think they were few' – said Büsser – 'since they added the necessary personnel for an orthodox attack and this was an extremely difficult operation, that had to be resolved in two hours and that, in addition, had to attain that the British surrendered without fighting.'[17] Today we know that none of these premises was met, and that the British garrison defended itself tenaciously, faithful to their institutional culture. The Argentines had to regret some casualties in their own troops, despite the enormous disproportion of opposing forces.

Royal Marines (Naval Party 8901) surrender to Argentine forces on 2 April 1982. (Photo by Rafael Wollmann)

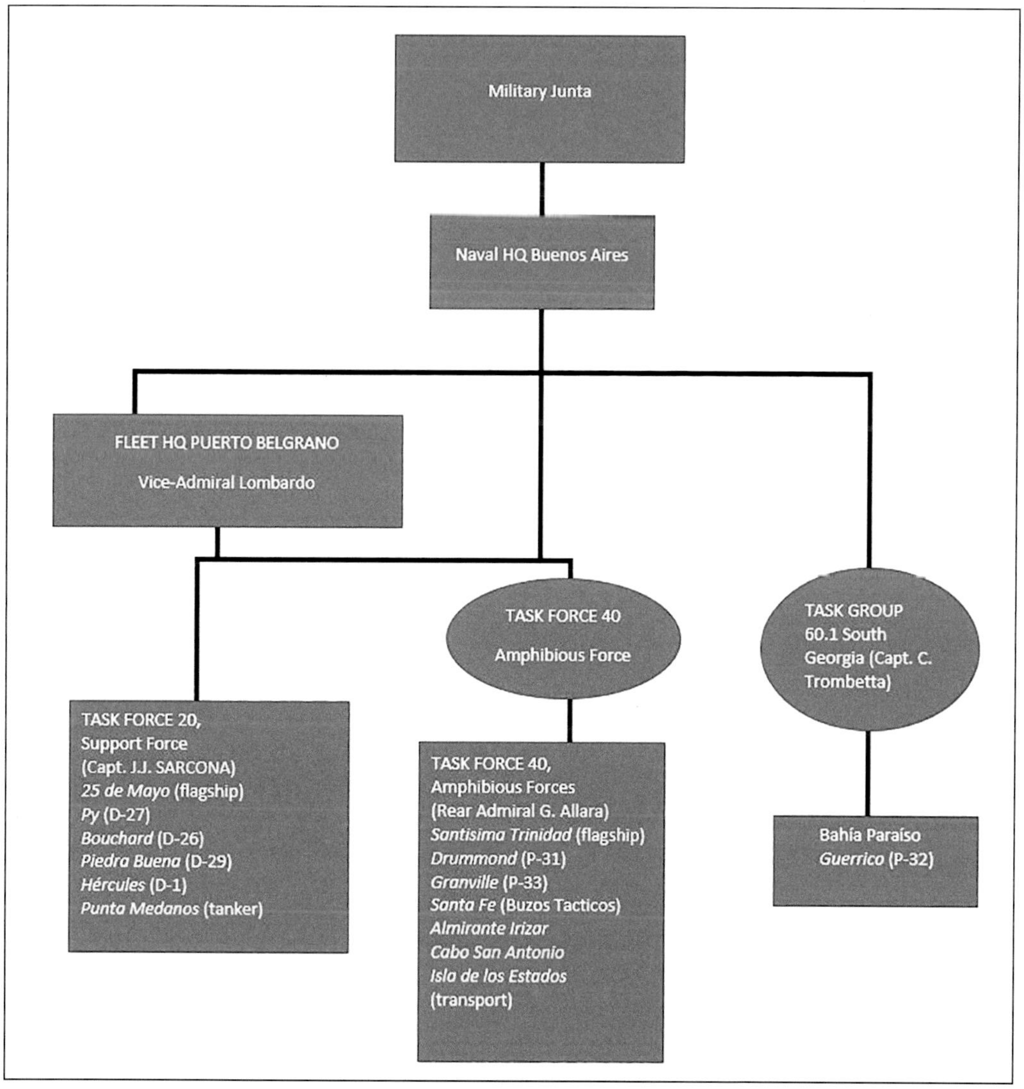

Argentine naval forces for Operation Azul, 28 March – 2 April 1982. (Diagram by Author)

The massive assault force – 904 men – knew that the Royal Marines were waiting for them, because they had intercepted radio transmissions from Port Stanley telling the population that a large fleet was approaching the islands, thus losing the element of surprise. This forced General Osvaldo Garcia (Commander of the Malvinas Theatre of Operations) and Rear Admiral Büsser (CAAF) to revise their original plan in transit to the target. The 25th Infantry Regiment (Lieutenant Colonel Mohamed Seineldín, initially in charge of the capture of the governor's house) was now assigned the objective of capturing the airport and clearing the runway. The mixed group of 16 amphibious commandos and tactical divers (Lieutenant Commander Pedro Giachino) was relieved of his original target of securing strategic points in Stanley, and instead was assigned the mission to capture Government House, with a force half the size of the defenders they had to face – although he did not know it at the time.

Inexplicably, the target of the bulk of the Argentine Marines appointed to take Naval Party 8901 HQ at Moody Brook was not altered, although it should have been anticipated that they would have been already deployed, and that they would no longer be caught with their pants down, as originally planned. They should instead have been redirected to Government House – to reinforce Giachino's group – a place that had become the concentration point of nearly all the British troops on the island.

The surrender of the governor, Rex Hunt and of Naval Party 8901 was not a true example of the current doctrine. The description made by Rear Admiral Büsser on this unique episode for an Argentine naval officer,

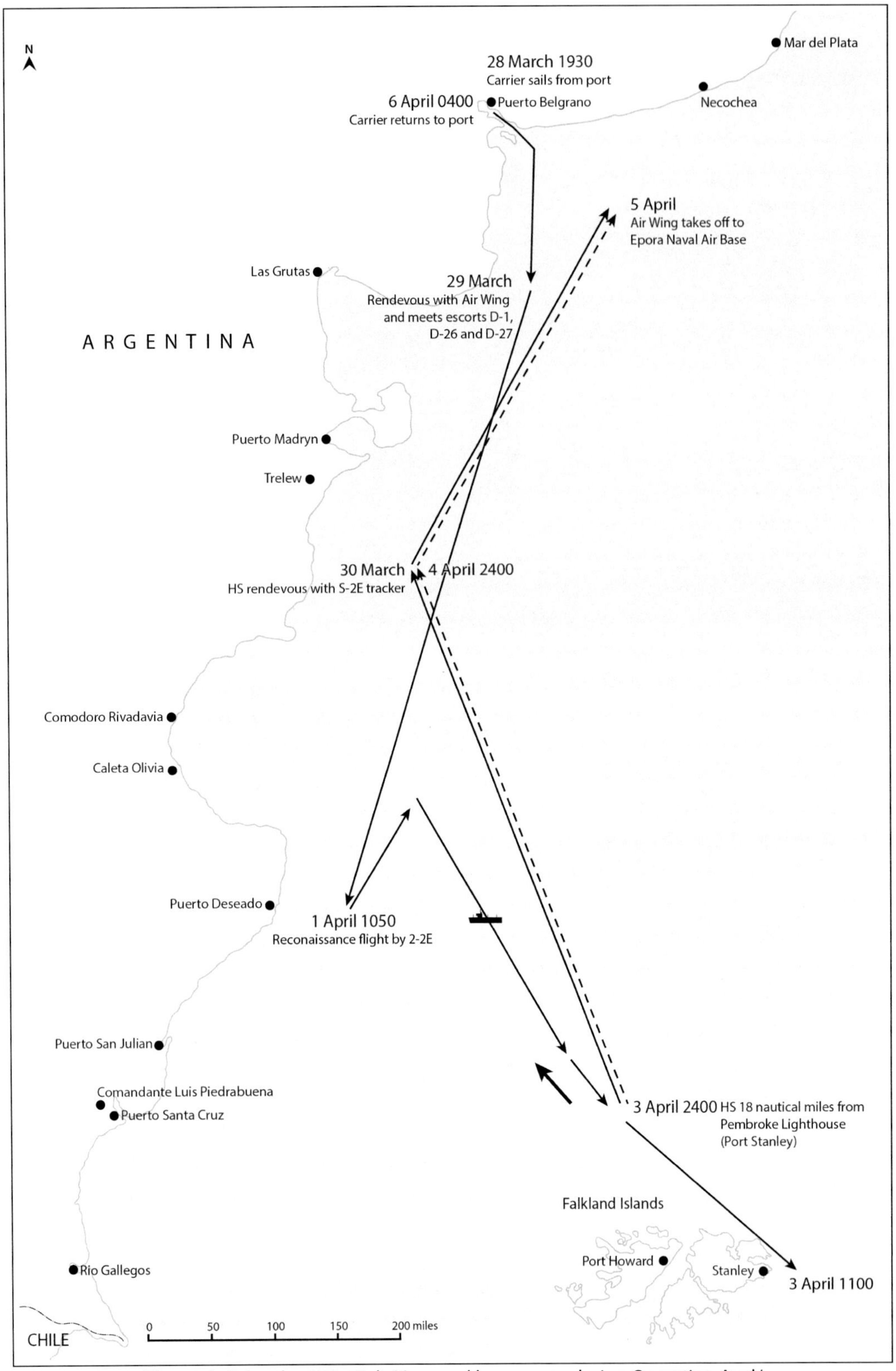

The route taken by ARA *25 de Mayo* and her escorts during Operation Azul/Rosario, between 28 March and 6 April 1982. (Map by George Anderson)

Although a closely guarded secret, a few Argentine Marine officers wanted to execute the entire British garrison to avenge the loss of their CO, a much respected and admired commando. The more senior Marine officers had to put all their authority and energy and managed to convince them to refrain from doing so, in the context that British casualties should be avoided at all costs. After the conflict, this merited the following reflection by Vice Admiral Lombardo: 'We had no experience in warfare; neither in the Falklands[/Malvinas] nor in South Georgia did we make the enemy sign a surrender document. They [the British] did it in every case.'[19] In defence of Büsser it should be said that he had not been given any specific instructions on how to proceed once the surrender of the governor was secured, so it should be concluded that the procedure followed on that occasion was delivered to his own professional criterion.

gives the impression of having been handled with some degree of improvisation and not within the protocols that should govern in time of war. Indeed, Büsser himself admits that it was a big mistake to have entered Government House – full of Royal Marines, alone and unarmed – and then shake hands with 20 or 30 enemy soldiers who minutes before had killed no other than one of his best tactical commanders – Commander Giachino.[18] Common sense indicated to force an unconditional surrender of the enemy garrison and, once this was achieved to his satisfaction, secure the perimeter and later make the governor sign the corresponding document of surrender.

Grytviken, South Georgia

Grytviken is an old whaling station on South Georgia Island, considered by the British a dependency of the Falklands/Malvinas which served as the seat of the colonial authority of the islands. It is located 1,500 km from Port Stanley. In 1982 there was a scientific base manned by the British Antarctic Survey at King Edward Point. This base was due to be dismantled in July for lack of government funds.

The assault on Grytviken on 3 April 1982 by Task Force 60.1 showed even greater shortcomings than Operation Azul/Rosario. Although the mission was also successful, it is considered a clear example of what happens when the organisation deviates from the pre-established doctrine and sound professional criteria. No other conclusion can be inferred by the number of casualties involved – four marines dead and two wounded – and the serious damage suffered by the A-69-class corvette ARA *Guerrico* (hull humber P-32; Commander Carlos Alfonso) and the destruction of a Puma helicopter of the Argentine Army operating from ARA *Bahia Paraiso* (Commander Ismael Garcia).[20]

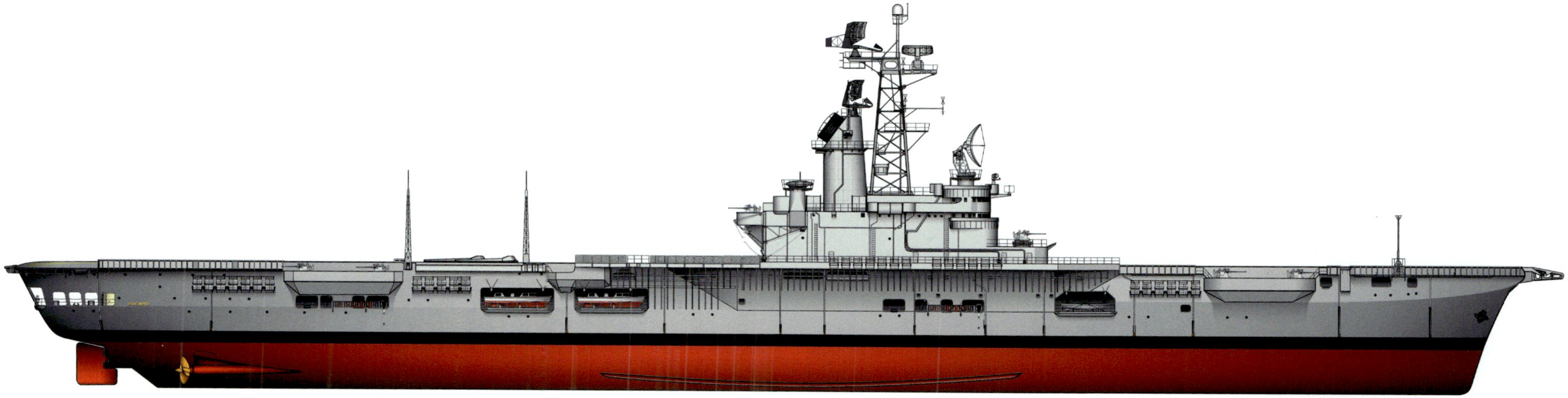

The centrepiece and pride of the Argentine Navy as of 1982 was the aircraft carrier ARA *25 de Mayo* (V-2). Constructed as a Colossus-class aircraft carrier and commissioned into the Royal Navy as HMS *Venerable* (R63) during the final months of the Second World War, in 1948 she was sold to the Netherlands and renamed HNLMS *Karel Doorman*. Following a comprehensive rebuild, in 1955-1958, she saw service during the Dutch-Indonesian stand-off over Western New Guinea in 1960-1962, and then ran anti-submarine patrols in the North Atlantic with NATO. After a boiler room fire in 1968, the carrier was sold to Argentina where her air group consisted of A-4Q Skyhawks, S-2 Trackers, and S.61 Sea King helicopters. (Artwork by Ivan Zajac)

In 1955-1958, while still serving with the Royal Netherlands Navy, HNLMS *Karel Doorman* was rebuilt with an 8° angled deck, new elevators, a new island, equipped with 40mm anti-aircraft guns and a steam catapult, and received entirely new aviation facilities and electronics (including a Dutch-built radar). Her last pre-Falklands refit took place in 1981 resulting in the flight deck as reconstructed here, including an upgrade of the arrestor gear, steam catapult and the forward edge of the port-side angled deck – all aimed to enable her to operate Super Etendards. Catapult-related issues prevented her from doing so and thus the ship still served during the Falklands/Malvinas War equipped with A-4Qs, T-2s and S.61s. Notable are the positions for a total of ten 40mm anti-aircraft guns, including four to the fore, four to the aft and one each to the fore and aft of the island. (Artwork by Ivan Zajac)

Constructed as a Brooklyn-class cruiser and commissioned into the US Navy as USS *Phoenix* (CL-46) in 1938, the future ARA *General Belgrano* (C-4) survived the Japanese attack on Pearl Harbour and then the Second World War in the Pacific. Decommissioned on 3 July 1946, she was sold to Argentina on 9 April 1951 and re-commissioned as ARA *17 Octubre* on 17 October 1951, but then renamed ARA *General Belgrano* in 1956. In 1967-68, she underwent her last major upgrade, which included the installation of new Dutch radars (Signaal LW-02 or -03 on foremast, and DA-01 or -02 on the aft mast). Two launchers for Sea Cat anti-aircraft missiles were installed (one on either side of the bridge), and the original fore Mk.33 director for 127mm guns replaced by a fire control radar for missiles. Primary armament included fifteen 6-inch (152mm) guns in five turrets, eight 5-inch (127mm) guns (installed amidships, below the funnels), and a single Alouette III helicopter housed inside the former aircraft hangar at the stern. The ship retained two quad and two twin 40mm Bofors 40/60 anti-aircraft guns and 10 twin 20mm guns, but it remains unclear how many of these were still aboard as of 1982. The ship was sunk by HMS *Conqueror* on 2 May 1982, with the loss of 321 crewmembers and two civilians: 772 other crewmembers were rescued over the following three days. (Artwork by Ivan Zajac)

Ordered on 18 May 1970 and completed on 10 May 1976 at the Vickers Shipbuilding yard in Barrow-in-Furness, UK, ARA *Hercules* (D-1) was constructed as a Type 42 destroyer, and delivered to Argentina on 19 September 1977. Generally identical to the initial Type 42 units commissioned by the Royal Navy, she was unique in having four launchers for MM38 Exocet anti-ship missiles (two of which are visible in this reconstruction, directly below and slightly ahead of the funnel). Her sister ship, ARA *Santisima Trinidad* (D-2) was intended to also receive Exocets but these do not appear to have been fitted. Other armament included a single 4.5-inch (114mm) gun in the front turret, a single launcher with twin rails for Sea Dart anti-aircraft missiles, two 20mm anti-aircraft guns and six tubes for 12.75-inch (324mm) anti-submarine torpedoes. The COAN took care to buy two Westland Lynx HAS.Mk 23 anti-submarine helicopters for them, and these took part in Operation Rosario, supporting the landings in a variety of ways (the example with serial 3-H-142 crashed into the sea near *Santisima Trinidad*, on 2 May 1982). (Artwork by Ivan Zajac)

Launched on 21 May 1944 and commissioned into the US Navy as USS *Hank* (DD-702) on 28 August 1944, the future ARA *Segui* was a destroyer of the Allen M. Sumner-class – perhaps the best US-designed destroyer of the Second World War. The ship served during the Korean War and the Cuban Missile Crisis before being decommissioned and sold to Argentina on 1 July 1972. In service with the Argentine Navy, the ship retained her main armament of six 127mm guns (installed in three turrets), but the secondary armament of 40mm Bofors 40/60 guns was gradually decreased, and her ten 21in (533mm) torpedo tubes replaced by four launchers for MM38 Exocets (installed on an elevated platform around the forward funnel) and a three-tube launcher for anti-submarine torpedoes (between the two funnels). Finally, the two depth charge racks were retained on the stern. ARA *Segui* took part in Operation Rosario but then saw no action for the rest of the war. The ship was used to make tests for an improvised coastal Exocet battery, which later was used in an attack that hit HMS *Glamorgan*, off Port Stanley, on 12 June 1982. ARA *Segui* was scrapped in 1983. (Artwork by Ivan Zajac)

Another vessel of the Allen M. Sumner-class acquired by Argentina was the former USS *Borie* (DD-704) of the US Navy, originally commissioned on 21 September 1944. Following service in the Pacific, the Korean War, the Mediterranean and during the Cuban Missile Crisis and the Vietnam Wars, this destroyer was modified through addition of a Drone Antisubmarine Helicopter (DASH) system, before being decommissioned in June 1972. The Argentine Navy acquired it later the same year and renamed it ARA *Bouchard* (D-26), after a famous privateer. While the ship lost all of her torpedo tubes and light artillery armament, in 1977-1978 four launchers for MM38 Exocets were installed between the funnels. ARA *Bouchard* saw intensive service during the Falklands/Malvinas War of 1982. It escorted the carrier ARA *25 de Mayo* during the initial invasion, and then – together with sister ship ARA *Piedra Buena* – ARA *Belgrano* on 2 May 1982, when the latter was sunk. ARA *Bouchard* may have been hit on that occasion by a British Mk. 8 torpedo that failed to detonate. On 16 May, ARA *Bouchard* engaged a submarine off the Rio Grande Naval Base, while during the night from 17 to 18 May, her radars detected a Sea King helicopter from HMS *Invincible* as this was approaching the Argentine coast on a mission to insert special forces: this forced the British crew to abandon the mission and fly to Chile instead, where the Sea King was deliberately destroyed to avoid a diplomatic incident. ARA *Bouchard* was sold for scrap in 1984. (Artwork by Ivan Zajac)

ARA *San Luis* (S-32) was one of only two operational submarines of Argentine Navy as of 1982. Constructed by Howaldtswerke Deutsche Werft in Germany to the 209-class design, this diesel-powered boat armed with eight 533mm (21in) torpedo tubes was commissioned into service on 24 May 1974 and proved a major problem for the Royal Navy during the early phases of the Falklands/Malvinas War. Although intensively prosecuted by British warships and helicopters, *San Luis* is known to have launched two attacks: on 1 May 1982 it fired a single SST-4 torpedo at frigates HMS *Brilliant* and HMS *Yarmouth* north of Port Stanley. Ten days later, it fired two SST-4s at frigates HMS *Alacrity* and HMS *Arrow*. All torpedoes missed due to problems with the fire-control computer which broke down at the beginning of the war, forcing the skipper to operate the weapons' system manually (or in 'emergency mode'). Moreover, all torpedoes fired cut their wire, making it impossible for the crew to guide them. Both problems were only solved after the end of the war. (Artwork by Ivan Zajac)

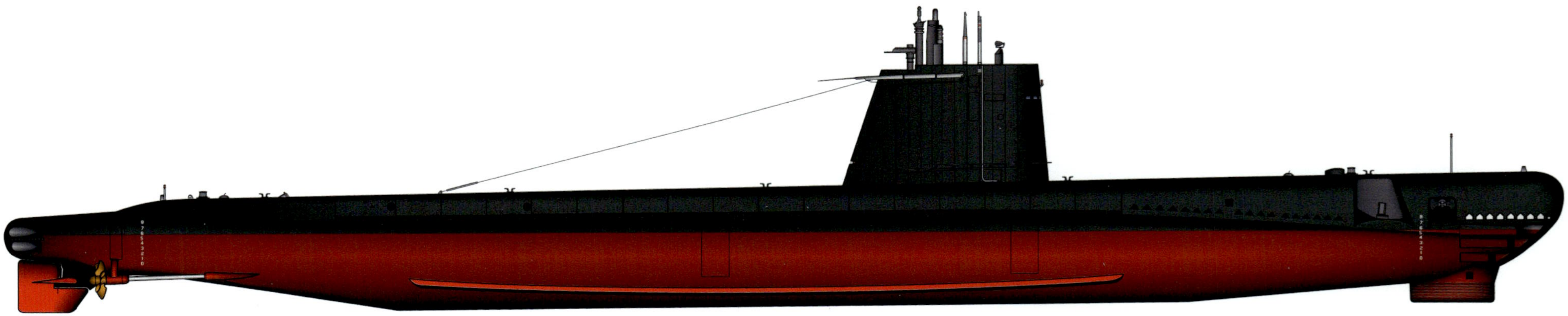

Originally constructed as USS *Catfish* (SS-339) of the Balao-class for the US Navy, and commissioned on 19 March 1945, this boat underwent the GUPPY II conversion in 1948-1949 (which provided her with greater submerged speed and endurance), and then served during the Korean and Vietnam wars. Argentina purchased it in 1971, and commissioned it under the name ARA *Santa Fe* (S-21) on 1 July 1971. Diesel-powered and armed with ten 21-inch (533) torpedo tubes (six forward and four aft), the sub never fired in anger: by 1982, it was in poor condition and only months short of being decommissioned. Nevertheless, it led the Argentine invasion of the Falklands by deploying tactical divers at Yorke Bay. On 17 April 1982, it departed from Mar del Plata to deploy a party of marines and supplies from Puerto Belgrano to Grytviken, in South Georgia. After accomplishing this mission, on 25 April *Santa Fe* was detected by helicopters of the Royal Navy while still on the surface, and attacked by depth charges, which caused extensive internal damage. Barely managing to return to Grytviken on the surface, it came under repeated attacks by additional helicopters, which prevented her crew from conducting repairs and diving again. Eventually, *Santa Fe* was abandoned by her crew while listing at Grytviken pier on South Georgia and was captured together with the Argentine garrison. (Artwork by Ivan Zajac)

The COAN acquired a total of 13 S-2A/E/Fs between 1954 and 1977, of which two S-2As served as US-2A utility transports, while three S-2Gs purchased after the Falklands conflict in 1994 were only used as sources of spares. The rest of the fleet – minus four written off in various accidents before 1982 – saw intensive operations during the Falklands War, even if the majority were deployed from bases on the Argentine mainland. A mix of S-2E/Fs – all painted in gull gray on upper surfaces and sides, and off-white on undersurfaces, wearing the Argentine Navy's insignia (a black anchor) as national insignia on their wings – was operated by 2nd Naval Anti-Submarine Squadron (badge shown in inset) from ARA *25 de Mayo*: the example shown here, 0705/2-AS-26 established the position of the Royal Navy's Task Force, late on 1 May 1982, while 0704/2-AS-24 became the only example to deploy a torpedo against a possible enemy submarine during the Falklands/Malvinas War. (Artwork by Tom Cooper)

The COAN acquired 16 refurbished A-4Bs in 1971-72, and they received the export designation A-4Q. All were operated by the 3rd Naval Fighter-Bomber Squadron. Ten were still around as of 1982, and eight were made operational and embarked aboard ARA *25 de Mayo* for Operation Rosario. On 1-2 May 1982, six were prepared for a strike on the Royal Navy's Task Force and each was armed with four Mk.82 bombs, but this mission was never launched. The example illustrated here – BuAerNo 144882, COAN serial 0654/3-A-301 – was scheduled to lead that attack while flown by the CO of the 3rd Squadron, Capitán de Corbeta Castro Fox. Subsequently, the aircraft was re-equipped for an air defence mission, armed with AIM-9B Sidewinder air-to-air missiles, attached directly to the main underwing pylons. (Artwork by Tom Cooper)

Another of the A-4Qs operational in 1982 was this example, BuAerNo 144929, COAN serial 0658/3-A-305. As per all the other Skyhawks of the Argentine Navy, it was painted in gull gray on top surfaces and sides – frequently bleached into a 'dirty white' by the elements and wear by 1982 – and off-white on undersurfaces. The aircraft was one of six prepared for the 'carrier battle' expected to take place on 1-2 May, and then took part in the squadron's attack on HMS *Ardent* on 21 May 1982 (during which it suffered light damage). It is shown as armed for these missions with four Mk.82 bombs, all equipped with Mk.12 Snakeye retarding fins, installed on a multiple ejector rack carried under the centreline. (Artwork by Tom Cooper)

Late in 1980 the 2nd Naval Fighter-Bomber Squadron, COAN – a unit that formerly flew North American T-28 Fennecs – was reformed and began the conversion process to be equipped with 14 Super Etendards, scheduled to replace the obsolete A-4Q Skyhawks. Due to the unplanned early start of Operation Rosario, and the resulting arms embargo, only the first five Super Etendards and five AM39 Exocets were in Argentina when the war of 1982 erupted. Nevertheless, the aircraft and missiles were made operational and deployed in combat, with devastating consequences for one of the Royal Navy's Type 42 destroyers, and one of its crucial logistics ships. The aircraft illustrated here took part in the attack on HMS *Sheffield* on 4 May and in the disputed mission against HMS *Invincible* on 30 May 1982, and wore corresponding 'kill' markings applied on the forward fuselage (shown inset, together with the unit badge). The bottom inset shows an AM39. (Artwork by Tom Cooper)

The third most important type embarked on board ARA *25 de Mayo* as of 1982 was the Sikorsky S-61D-4 Sea King (export variant of the SH-3D), five of which were operated by the 2nd Naval Helicopter Squadron (badge shown inset). As in US Navy service, they were painted in white on top surfaces and sides, and light gull gray on undersides, but also received large serials identifying the operating unit and individual airframes. During the war Sea Kings were used for long-range search and rescue, surveillance and for casevac, which is why this example has large red crosses. On 31 May 1982, this helicopter – serial 2-H-234, and its sister 2-H-233 – took part in a daring rescue mission from Rio Grande to recover crucial naval personnel from Pebble Island. (Artwork by Goran Sudar)

As of 2 April 1982, the 2nd Naval Helicopter Squadron, COAN had nine Alouette IIIs and two Lynx HAS.Mk 23s on strength, and nearly all were embarked aboard ships during the subsequent capture of the Falkland Islands and South Georgia. This example – serial 3-H-110 – was embarked aboard the Antarctic supply ship ARA *Bahia Paraiso* and played a leading role in the success of the landings on 3 April 1982. During the conflict, all of COAN's Alouettes wore disruptive camouflage patterns, usually in dark tan or light brown and one or two shades of green, applied in wrap-around fashion. Only one such helicopter was lost: the example embarked on ARA *Belgrano*. (Artwork by Tom Cooper)

A-4Q serial number 3-A-304 about to 'catch the wire' on landing aboard ARA *25 de Mayo*. Notable in the background to the right is the 'LSO-platform', with multiple landing signal officers responsible for helping the pilot land on the short, narrow and constantly moving deck of the aircraft carrier. (via Tom Cooper)

A rare colour photograph of the destroyer ARA *Bouchard* (D-26), probably taken in 1979. Notable are two launchers for MM38 Exocets installed beside the funnels. This was one of two destroyers escorting ARA *Belgrano* at the time of its sinking. (Argentine Navy Photo)

ARA *Hercules* seen during high-speed trials. Notable in between the forward 114mm (4.5in) gun turret and the bridge is the launcher for Sea Dart anti-aircraft missiles, with two rounds (both painted in red) in position. Visible further to the rear, beneath the funnel, are two launchers for MM38 Exocet missiles – as installed only on this Type 42 destroyer constructed for the Argentine Navy. (Argentine Navy)

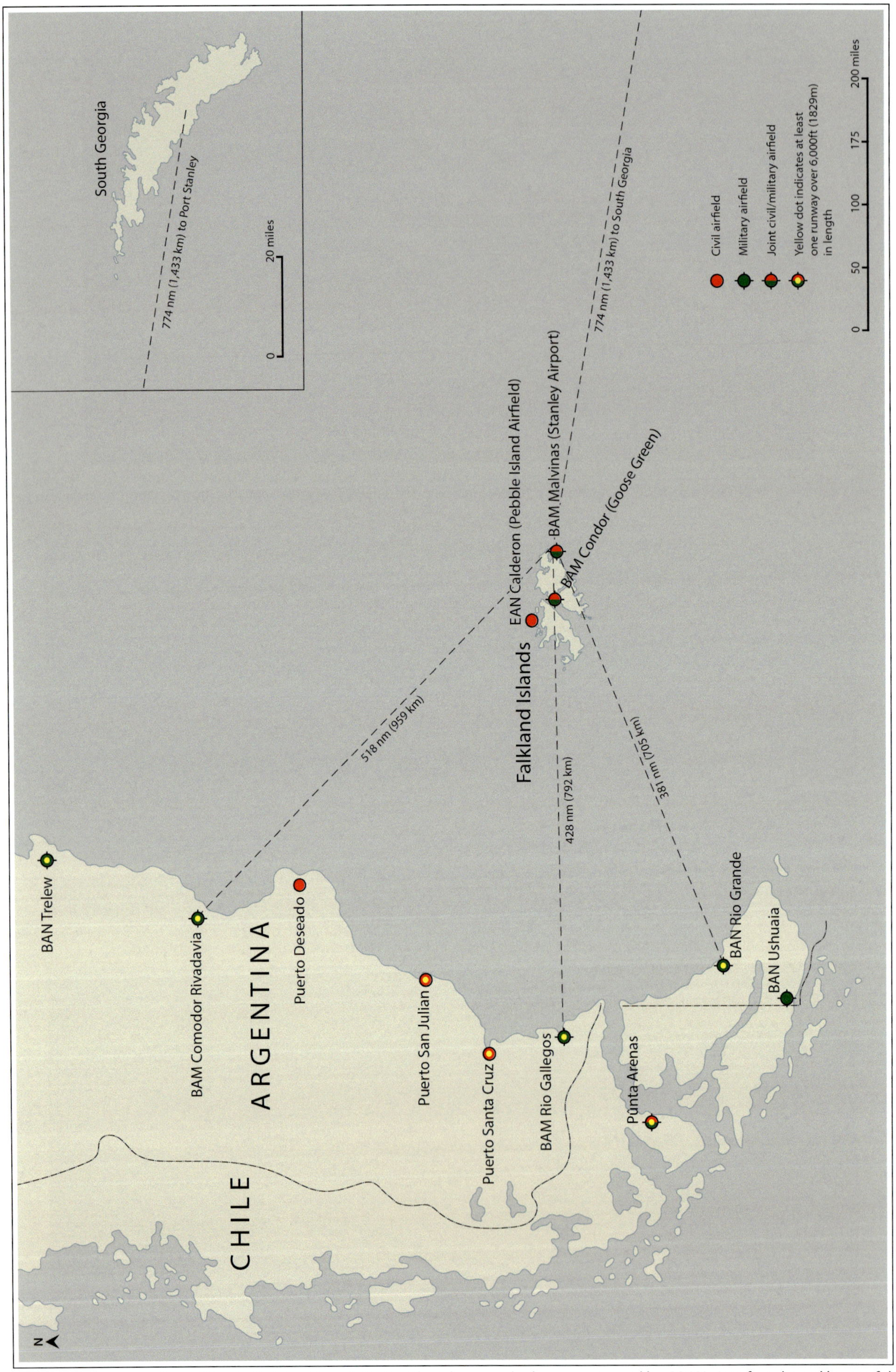

A map of the conflict zone of the Falklands/Malvinas War of 1982, with air bases and other airports used by COAN aircraft and naval bases of the Argentine Navy. Notably, official designations of Naval Air Bases of the Argentine Naval Aviation were prefixed with BAN, which is an abbreviation for Base Aeronaval. As of March 1982, these were BAN Comandante Espora (Bahia Blanca), home base of the 2nd and 3rd Naval Wings, with a runway of 8,500ft; BAN Almirante Zar (Trelew), home base of the 6th Naval Wing, with a runway of 8,400ft; and BAN Ushuaia (Tierra del Fuego Province), a small airfield adjacent to the local naval facilities, with a runway of only 4,600ft. No aircraft were operated from BAN Ushuaia during the Falklands/Malvinas War. (Map by George Anderson)

Polar Ship *Bahia Paraiso* (9,200 tons) in Cumberland Bay. Contrary to many British versions this ship was completely unarmed. (Argentine Navy)

Corvette ARA *Guerrico* (P-32) which took part in the South Georgia operation, was fitted with four Exocet MM38 anti-ship missiles of 42 km range. (Argentine Navy)

The commander of the Argentine Task Force lost the tactical surprise when he established communication with the base commander of the British Antarctic Survey (BAS) in King Edward Cove to reveal his intentions, which allowed the enemy to adopt defensive dispositions that ultimately proved devastating for the Argentine Marines. Additionally, he ignored a signal from fleet HQ informing him of the presence of 22 Royal Marines in the area and disregarded the explicit warning made by Stephen Martin (head of the BAS personnel) that there was a military presence in the base, which had orders from the British government to resist should the Argentines land. These warnings should have given the CO of the Task Group a clear indication that he could envisage some kind of opposition – as had already occurred on 2 April in the Falklands/Malvinas, where Argentine troops had had a large numerical superiority, an advantage that was not available in this occasion.

In addition to this important handicap, it must be mentioned the inadequate composition of the Argentine Task Group for the mission assigned. In the first place, the polar ship ARA *Bahia Paraiso* lacked any kind of armament and the frigate ARA *Guerrico* did not have her artillery in proper operating order due to the sub-Antarctic climate, nor did the helicopters employed have a combat configuration. This entire new scenario imposed upon the Argentine forces precautions much greater than normal, to avoid material damage and unnecessary casualties from the enemy.

However, the Task Force CO disregarded all precautions and decided to expose the ARA *Guerrico* to the enemy's concentrated fire by ordering her penetration in broad daylight into King Edward Cove. This made the corvette an easy target for automatic weapons: *Guerrico* attracted a considerable volume of small-arms fire, which killed an NCO and seriously wounded five others – including a midshipman that lost one eye, later Rear Admiral (now retired) Ricardo Pingitore – and one of the launchers for MM38 Exocets was hit by a 66mm unguided rocket. The current doctrine imposed the use of the ship to provide the troops with naval gunfire support from outside the cove, taking tactical advantage of the extended range provided by the ship´s powerful artillery, adjusting her shots according to the requirements of the marines already landed.

The Argentine Marines were given the direct order to carry out the assault in broad daylight, even though the theatre of operations did not favour concealment. The assault was carried out without having previously identified the strength and location of the enemy and lacking adequate coordination – due to faulty communications – between the inter-service squads that had already landed, all of which violated elementary rules of common sense.

The organisational culture then in force delegated overall command of this operation to the senior naval officer on the spot – that is, the CO of the Naval Antarctic Squadron (a captain). However, his lack of expertise in this type of amphibious landing was quickly realised by his subordinates, who found themselves face to face with the enemy without a clear strategy to follow and

Alouette III helicopter (3-H-110) on board ARA *Bahia Paraiso* in Cumberland Bay. The pilot, First Lt. Remo Busson, was later able to rescue the entire crew of the Army Puma helicopter which had been shot down by enemy fire. (Rear Admiral retired Ricardo Pingitore)

Close-up of the bridge of corvette ARA *Guerrico*. Notable are two launchers for MM38 Exocets, one of which was hit by a 66mm rocket: much of the superstructure also received a large volume of British small-arms fire. (Argentine Navy)

total confusion within the ranks. The few squads that managed to land were momentarily pinned down by enemy´s small-arms fire; a Puma helicopter was heavily damaged while trying to land near the enemy´s position, but miraculously managed to make an emergency landing on the other side of the bay, thanks to the expert flying abilities of its pilot.

The senior Marine officer on board (a first lieutenant) was not consulted on the best way to tackle the enemy troops on land; this eventually led to an uncoordinated assault with an overexposure of the surface ships and a misuse of the strength of the Marine Corps, which ultimately revealed not only the absence of adequate planning, but also lack of professional criteria in the orders given by the CO of the Task Group.[21] Despite this organisational failure the mission ended in a narrow triumph – snatched from the edge of disaster.[22]

Many years after the end of the conflict the former CO of the frigate ARA *Guerrico*, the late Vice Admiral Alfonso, concluded in regard of the aforementioned operation:

> It is imperative, in spite of our excellent and natural ability to improvise, to know in advance the operational order, and that such order includes alternatives, sufficiently flexible in case of unexpected opposition. This becomes paramount when there are inter-service units of different capacities and from different branches of the navy involved. This approach especially applies if the operation to be carried out is not common for any of the members of the Task Group.[23]

A Fleet-in-Being Strategy

On 6 April 1982 the Argentine Navy informed the Junta – acting in its capacity as Military Committee – about its concept of the strategic manoeuvre to be developed in the theatre of operations. Vice Admiral Lombardo, as Commander of the South Atlantic Theatre of Operations (SATO), pointed out that the use of the Navy's surface fleet would be carried out only in favourable opportunities, as the very modest Argentine fleet had no capacity to confront the much larger and modern British Task Force and, therefore, their freedom of action would be restricted. He further added that the threat of nuclear attack submarines – whose number and location were unknown – made the indiscriminate use of surface ships risky, and that such a risk was only acceptable in the presence of profitable targets. This opportunity would present itself at the critical moment in which the enemy divided his forces or was engaged in an amphibious landing.[24] The latter hypothesis was deactivated when General Mario Menéndez informed his superiors that 'if the enemy landed in an undefended place, he was not in a position to repel them and push them back into the sea.'[25] This left the Navy only one option: to attack enemy ships before the landing occurred, for – if it was done during the landing – the chances of eliminating or stopping the invading British forces was simply impossible without support from the Argentine land forces. No matter how important any naval action may be, the end result of a war is always settled on land. In this case, a naval strike that would have interfered with the landing without being coordinated with the local defending army would not have yielded any positive results, as it ultimately happened.

The Alouette III helicopter piloted by Lieutenant Remo Busson, which operated from *Bahia Paraiso*, was deployed to successfully rescue the crew and troops from the Army Puma helicopter that was shot down near Grytviken harbour in April 1982. (Argentine Navy)

Submarine ARA *Santa Fe* (S-21) submerging in the South Atlantic Ocean near Mar del Plata in 1981. (Photo by Daniel Martin)

Likewise, the Argentine admirals shared the idea that 'Victory in combat does not always belong to the strongest party, it often leans in favour of the fleet that is quicker to react with boldness and audacity in order to face unforeseen events, and to seize the best opportunities.'[28] This had occurred, for example, in the Battle of Midway when the weaker American naval force succeeded in defeating the much powerful combined Japanese fleet. Could the Argentines achieve this in the South Atlantic?

There is no doubt that Vice Admiral Lombardo had to face an extremely difficult strategic situation, not only because he had to deal with a much stronger and larger enemy fleet than his own, but also a bold enemy that had the explicit support of the American and Chilean armed forces. Despite this, the Argentine Naval High Command never ruled out offensive actions that could disrupt the enemy´s naval power. This is what Vice Admiral Lombardo´s memoirs suggest, when he says: 'I never hesitated to order a strike when I was convinced that with it, I could cause damage or disruption to the enemy. I did not hesitate to risk ships, planes or soldiers, that was my duty, and my responsibility as Chief of Naval Operations.'[29] However, Vice Admiral Lombardo's means were very limited, and so was the damage he could inflict on the enemy at sea.

The mere fact of having an aircraft carrier capable of launching an air strike on the Royal Navy's Task Force was something that unnerved the British high command throughout the campaign. In her memoirs, British Prime Minister Margaret Thatcher said:

> The trouble was that we knew that their ships might break out again, and we might not find them quickly enough to stop them. Again, it was the Argentine aircraft carrier ARA *25 de Mayo* which was the main threat. I had been told that if possible, we needed to deal with their aircraft carrier before the landing, but most of the time we had been unable to find it.[30]

The naval campaign showed that *control of the sea* is a relative and not absolute thing. Although the British showed a greater calling to control it, they never achieved it completely, especially as regards the naval aspect of the campaign. The British Task Force lacked

This approach adopted by the Argentine Navy to solve the strategic riddle that posed the control of the sea around the Falklands/Malvinas – or deny it to the enemy – perfectly reflected the dominant beliefs within the institution.

The Argentine Naval High Command knew that the sea conditions and the imminent arrival of the winter in the South Atlantic created a very narrow window of opportunity for the British to capture the islands. The British fleet could not sustain operations in the South Atlantic for an indefinite time. As Alastair Finlan rightly concluded: 'The campaign to regain the Falklands[/Malvinas] was fought on a very narrow margin of error and a tight timescale. The element of fortune was very high and the gulf between winning and losing was extremely narrow.'[26]

After the sinking of the ARA *General Belgrano* on 2 May – as already mentioned – the Navy adopted a fleet-in-being strategy. This concept is of particular value for a fleet which is inferior to that of its adversary – in quality or quantity – and which cannot objectively dispute or control the sea by the normal methods.[27]

Cruiser ARA *General Belgrano* in 1980. (Argentine Navy, with permission)

Guided missile destroyer ARA *Hercules* sometime after June 1980. Note the launchers for MM38 Exocets beside the funnel. (Photo Argentine Navy, with permission)

sufficient resources to achieve air supremacy; all it could aspire to was local air superiority, of limited intervals. The blockade of the Argentine garrison in the Falklands/Malvinas was not completely hermetic, because England lacked the naval superiority necessary for it and airborne early warning. In other words, control of the sea was never absolute. This essential factor should have been exploited by the Argentine Navy to give a greater respite to the local garrison defending the islands.

Many analysts wonder, even today, why the Argentine fleet did not go out again after the sinking of the cruiser ARA *General Belgrano*. Vice Admiral Lombardo was consulted after the conflict had ended as to whether a last action of the fleet had been considered towards the end of May. This was his response:

> No. We had no longer an operational fleet. *Belgrano* was sunk. *Veinticinco de Mayo* [*sic*] had no aircraft. The two type 42 [*sic*] destroyers were out of action, one had hit a rock [in reference to ARA *Hercules*], and the other was having engine troubles. We had no operational submarines. Our two old American WW II destroyers were only capable of making 15 knots. Our best tanker *Punta Medanos* was unserviceable and was being brought up from the South under tow. The only good modern ships we had left were the [corvettes] ARA *Drummond*, ARA *Granville* and ARA *Guerrico*. These were all at sea near Puerto Belgrano, and I asked Admiral Anaya if I could send them to intercept the British supply ships sailing between Ascension Island and the [Falklands/]Malvinas. But he said 'no', I was not to expand the conflict.[31]

In the light of the aforementioned facts, it is safe to say that the initiatives suggested by Vice Admiral Lombardo to form surface action groups to act offensively were vetoed by Admiral Anaya on the grounds that the conflict should not be expanded. In this context, the accusation made by the Rattenbach Commission after the conflict – in the sense that Admiral Lombardo 'failed to conceive an aggressive operational strategy'[32]seems a bit harsh, since this appreciation did not take into account the possibility of a veto by the Military Committee or the general state of the fleet at the end of May. Lastly, in Vice Admiral Lombardo's defence, it should be said that the Argentine Navy alone suffered 50 percent of the total casualties in the conflict, including officers, NCOs and conscripts, which hardly permits to sustain that the Navy eluded being in harm's way.

Change of command ceremony on board the submarine ARA *Santa Fe* in late December 1981. Lt Cdr Horacio Bicain (CO during the war) is the first on the right facing the camera. (Horacio Bicain)

Command and Control

At the top of the Argentine chain of command structure was the so-called Military Committee – none other than the ruling Junta – composed of the three commanders-in-chief of the three armed forces. This tripartite body was clearly unsuitable to exercise command and control and – in practice – operational command was vested in the South Atlantic Theatre of Operations (Commander Vice Admiral Lombardo) whose command headquarters was located in Puerto Belgrano Naval Base, near Bahia Blanca. However, he found multiple interference and overlapping responsibilities that prevented him from acting as a single operational commander. The Rattembach Report confirms that 'the Military Committee did not exercise the authority of which it was legally vested due to interferences that, to a greater or lesser degree, were produced by the commanders-in-chief according to its modalities, personality and customs'.

Vice Admiral Lombardo´s appointment to conduct the in-theatre operations in the Falklands/Malvinas conflict reveals Anaya's influence within the Junta. The former Chief of Naval Operations had been the first to learn of the Azul/Rosario plan, and had in many ways masterminded the operation. It was also clear that – as it was an island theatre of operations – the greatest effort would fall on the shoulders of the Navy. Furthermore, Vice Admiral Lombardo belonged to the subculture of submariners – a profession very well suited to direct naval operations against the British Task Force – whose greatest threat for the small Argentine fleet was represented by their hunter-killer nuclear attack boats.

From the very beginning, most of the strategic decisions were subordinated to the particular interest of each service. The South Atlantic Air Force Command (Fuerza Aérea Sur) never subordinated itself to the in-theatre commander; this resulted in the existence of two independent commands which operated separately in the same geographical area, most of the time without prior coordination. Throughout the conflict, this lack of command and control structure affected the combat striking power of the Argentine armed forces, especially in cases of reconnaissance flights, combat operations and search and rescue missions.

Vice Admiral Lombardo was a faithful representative of the institutional culture of the Navy. Late Captain Alejandro Tierno, who served many years as professor at the Argentine Naval War College recalls that 'it was a Navy where there was greater fear of the senior officers than of the enemy'.[33] This culture was responsible for most of his decisions which were made in solitude, with very sporadic interventions of his staff, for there was no experience in the Navy at the time – and there is none now – in directing a war through the use of a general staff – with the only exception of the war games held at the Naval War College.

As a result of this, he was criticised after the conflict over 'delays and excess of precautions in the use of maritime logistics, at the beginning of operations, by an overestimation of the naval blockade anounced by the enemy'.[34] Vice Admiral Lombardo – aware of the serious losses that could be inflicted by enemy nuclear submarines on his own merchant ships – had a conflict of conscience when faced with the decision to send civilians to the islands on unarmed ships in poor fighting conditions. In the event of being sunk their crews would have generated greater pressure on the domestic front. According to Vice Admiral Lombardo:

> The enemy capacity to strike in daylight or by night actions, through high-speed submarines and carrier-based attack helicopters and aircraft makes it almost impossible to supply the [Falkland/Malvinas] Islands by merchant shipping. Ships with a speed of no more than 16 knots will be exposed for many hours to enemy attack, even when they reach the islands themselves. If several vessels were sent simultaneously these could also be sunk and the rate of those who might arrive would be very small, and the loss of property and personnel very high and difficult to accept.[35]

The final draft of the campaign plan that Vice Admiral Lombardo communicated to General Menéndez established that the Falklands/Malvinas defence would not have naval support of any kind: this was considered impractical due to the lack of supply units. The few naval or air assets, lack of airborne early warning systems, and very modest elements of reconnaissance were the result of the absence of prior military planning, all of which greatly contributed to the enemy's freedom of action. Both contenders paid a heavy price for the always present inter-service rivalry. The British – to a greater extent than the Argentines – went far enough to achieve

Destroyer ARA *Bouchard* (D-26) of the Allen M Sumner-class (ex-USS *Borie*), was one of the two escorts of the *Belgrano* at the time of her sinking. (Argentine Navy Photo)

a good coordination and cooperation between the armed forces, particularly at the tactical level.

Surface Ship Operations

The somewhat low-profile role of the Argentine fleet during the conflict has perhaps generated the greatest controversy in naval circles worldwide. In analysing its performance, we should bear in mind the political and strategic context in which it had to operate and the serious limitations imposed by

1) the presence of enemy nuclear attack submarines,
2) the need to preserve a reserve naval capacity – as a defence against possible post-war Chilean aggression, and
3) the lack of adequate and sufficient intelligence and airborne early warning capability.

Having said this, we briefly summarise its deployment and actions until 4 May 1982. The Argentine surface fleet was what defence experts call a *balanced navy* in relation to its neighbours and potential rivals – the United Kingdom was not one of them – who

ARA *Belgrano* in the port of Ushuaia during the war. This is probably the last photo taken of her afloat. (Argentine Navy Photo)

were outperformed in training and discipline. The Argentine Navy could perform limited sea control operations, but it was by no means a modern fleet. It had been more than a century since it had had to participate in any naval action; it was aged, scarred and rigid. In early 1982 the fleet was going through a transition phase where new units – such as the British-built Type 42 destroyers and the brand new French A-69-class corvettes – coexisted with the oldest ones dating back to Second World War; this made it altogether weaker.

The core of the fleet was formed by its two capital ships, the light aircraft carrier ARA *25 de Mayo* of 15,892 tons of displacement – the 37-year-old former HMS *Venerable* bought from the Dutch Navy in 1969 – with a small air group embarked of eight Skyhawk A-4Q aircraft, and a Second World War era light cruiser, ARA *General Belgrano* – former USS Phoenix launched in 1938 and sold to Argentina in the early 1950s – that mounted fifteen 6-inch guns: this gave her, on paper, some advantage over the British guns, whose calibre was just 4.5 inches. It was thought that its old armour might protect her from anti-ship missiles.

ARA *Piedrabuena* (D-29) – ex-USS *Collett* – was the other escort of the cruiser *Belgrano* during her last war patrol. (Argentine Navy)

The German built submarine 209-class ARA *Salta* (S-31) sailing on the surface in 1979. Sister-boat, ARA *San Luis* (S-32), played an active role during the war. (Roberto Salinas)

In 1976, the surface-to-surface Exocet MM38 missile launchers were installed in three old Second World War vintage destroyers of American origin of the Allen M. Sumner-class (ARA *Bouchard*, ARA *Segui* and ARA *Piedrabuena*) and one of the Gearing-class (ARA *Py*) to give them greater anti-ship capability. In addition, one of the new Type 42 destroyers (ARA *Hercules*) and the A-69-class corvettes also had Exocet missile launchers.

Among the most modern units were the German built submarines of the 209-class such as ARA *San Luis* (Commander Fernando Azcueta) and ARA *Salta* (Commander Carlos Riveiro and Commander Roberto Salinas), assembled in sections in Argentine Navy Yards, which – although of conventional diesel-electric propulsion – were very quiet and very difficult to detect. They were manned by well-trained crews and equipped with modern SST-4 torpedoes that were still untested prototypes. However, the submarine force was tiny – despite being a capital weapon of the modern navies – since it had only four units, of which two (ARA *Santa Fe* and ARA *Santiago del Estero*) were old submersibles of the American vintage Guppy-class and were to be scraped shortly from active duty.

The Argentine fleet was under the direction of Rear Admiral Gualter Allara, a rather short man with a compact figure, of dynamic and intelligent personality, who enjoyed great prestige within the service. His superior officer, Vice Admiral Lombardo, held him with great personal and professional regard. He had graduated in the top 3 percent from the Naval Academy in 1951 – 4th of 135 officers. In 1978 he had been appointed Deputy Secretary of Foreign Affairs and a year later he exercised command of the aircraft carrier ARA *25 de Mayo*, so he was perfectly aware of its operational advantages and limitations. During 1980-1981 he was appointed Chairman of the Argentine Naval Commission in Europe based in London – a key post which made him familiar with the British role in NATO. As a result, when presented with the enemy's capabilities to deploy its fleet in the South Atlantic, he was unconvinced that the UK would withdraw nuclear submarines from the North Atlantic in the midst of the Cold War.[36]

On paper the Argentine fleet posed a serious threat to the Royal Navy and, in favourable circumstances – if well directed – it could damage the British naval strategy, particularly during the amphibious landing stage.

Task Force 79

As already mentioned, the Argentine surface fleet could not engage in a decisive battle, in order to avoid unnecessary losses that could not be replaced at short notice to continue the fighting.

The almost certain presence in the theatre of operations of enemy nuclear attack submarines conditioned the deployment of the fleet, but did not prevent Rear Admiral Allara, who hoisted his flag on the aircraft carrier ARA *25 de Mayo* (Captain José Sarcona), from splitting his forces into three task groups, keeping them well to the northwest of the Falklands/Malvinas, outside the Total Exclusion Zone, waiting to strike.

This deployment of the Argentine surface units was intended to anticipate and eventually neutralise the expected British amphibious landing somewhere on the islands. All ships of the Argentine fleet in seaworthy condition had been at sea since mid-April, training for the almost certain encounter with the enemy fleet.

After the fall of South Georgia to the British on 26 April it became apparent to the Argentine Naval High Command that the British had naval forces in the South Atlantic. It was about this time that a warning was received – which was in reality false – that HMS *Exeter* (D89), a Type 42 destroyer forward deployed in Belize, had been seen in the company of a tanker crossing the Panama Canal towards the Pacific Ocean.

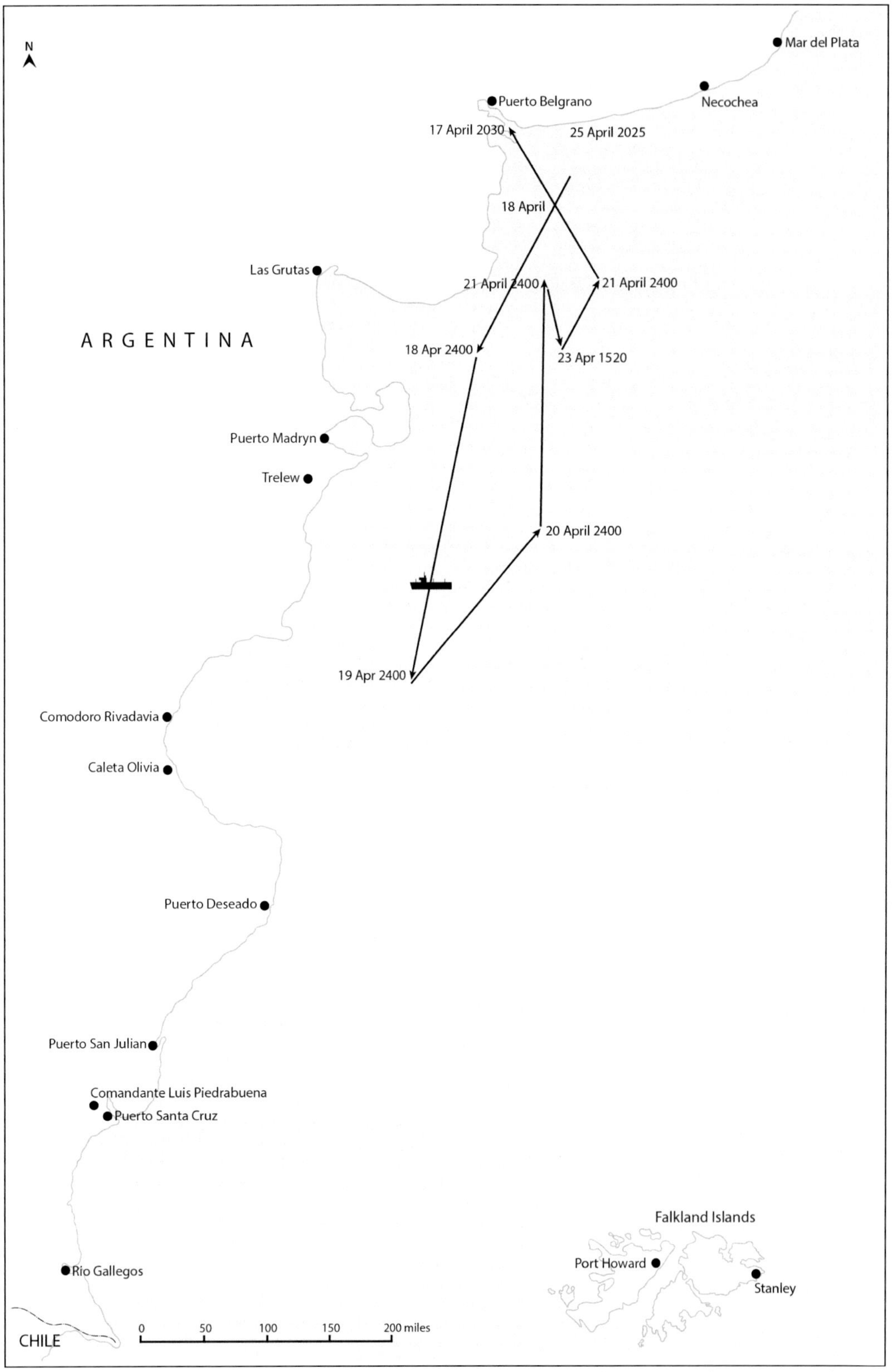

Route taken by ARA *25 de Mayo* during its short cruise from 17 to 25 April 1982. (Map by George Anderson)

Argentine ships operated under the generic designation of Task Force 79. As a result of the evolution of the naval situation in the theatre of operations, it was arranged towards 30 April to divide the fleet into three groups, as listed in Table 3.

On 1 May, when reports received in Naval HQ suggested that the British had started hostilities with air strikes on Port Stanley and Goose Green, the Argentine fleet saw an opportunity to surprise the enemy and hopefully knock out one of its capital ships. For the first time since Second World War, two fleets faced each other with aircraft carriers.

The three Task Forces were ordered to head towards the estimated position of the enemy fleet. They did so cautiously, steaming outside the perimeter of the British Total Exclusion Zone, waiting for a favourable opportunity to strike. Although the Argentines were unaware of it at the time, Task Group 79.3 operating in the south had already been located by the nuclear attack submarine HMS *Conqueror* (hull number S-48; Commander Chris Wreford-Brown).

However, it was far to the north that there was the greatest chance of a confrontation between the fleets. The British carriers had approached less than 100 miles off the coast of

Destroyer ARA *Hercules* (D-1) was the most modern warship of the Argentine fleet in 1982 together with her sister ship *Santisima Trinidad* (D-2). (Argentine Navy)

Task Force 79

Ship name	Type	Commissioned in Argentine Navy	Displacement	Armament	Exocet Launchers	No	Range	Speed	Complement	CO
ARA *25 de Mayo*	Aircraft Carrier	15.10.1968	19.896 Tons	Variable complement of S2E Trackers, A4Q Skyhawks, Sea King ASW helicopters, and A103 Alouette III helicopters		V-2	12.000 miles at 14 knots	20 knots	1500 men	CN José Sarcona
ARA *General Belgrano*	Light Cruiser	12.04.1951	13.645 Tons	15-6 inch (153 mm), 8-5 inch (127 mm), 25 cal, 2 twin 40mm, 1 Alouette III helicopter		C-4	7600 mil es at 15 knots	20 knots	1093 men	CN Héctor Bonzo
ARA *Hércules*	Type 42 destroyer	12.07.1976	4075 Tons	Missile Launchers: 1 Sea Dart (twin), 1- 4.5 in automatic, 2 – 20mm Oerlikon.A/S weapons: 6 Mk 32 (2 triple) torpedo tubes. 1 Sea Lynx helicopter	4 Exocet MM38 since 6.1980 (this was the only type 42 ever to be fitted with Exocet)	D-1	4000 miles at 18 knots	29 knots	300 men	CF Enrique Molina Pico
ARA *Santísima Trinidad*	Type 42 destroyer	1978	4075 Tons	Missile Launchers: 1 Sea Dart (twin), 1- 4.5 in automatic, 2 – 20mm Oerlikon.A/S weapons: 6 Mk 32 (2 triple) torpedo tubes. 1 Sea Lynx helicopter		D-2	4000 miles at 18 knots	29 knots	300 men	CF José Tejo
ARA *Seguí*	Allen M. Summer Class Destroyer	1.07.1972	3.320 Tons	4-3 inch ASW 6 (2 triple) Mk 32 torpedo tubes	4 Exocet MM38	D-25	4600 miles at 15 knots	31 knots	331 men	CF Néstor Fernandez Marasco
ARA *Bouchard*	Allen M. Summer Class Destroyer	1.07.1972	3.320 Tons	6-5 inch (127mm) ASW 6 (2 triple) Mk 32 torpedo tubes	4 Exocet MM38	D-26	4600 miles at 15 knots	31 knots	291 men	CF Washington Bárcena
ARA *Py*	Gearing Class Destroyer	13.02.1973	3532 Tons	6-5 inch (127mm) ASW 6 (2 triple) Mk 32 torpedo tubes	4 Exocet MM38	D-27	6150 at 11 knots	30 knots	200 men	CF Alberto Miqueleiz
ARA *Piedra Buena*	Allen M. Summer Class Destroyer	17,05.1977	3.320 Tons	6-5 inch (127mm) ASW 6 (2 triple) Mk 32 torpedo tubes	4 Exocet MM38	D-29	4600 miles at 15 knots	31 Knots	180 men	CF Horacio Grassi
ARA *Drummond*	French A-69 Class Corvette	9.11.1978	1250 Tons	1-100/55 mm, 1-40/70 mm, 2-20mm, ASW 2 Mk32 torpedo tubes	4 Exocet MM38	P-31	4500 miles at 14 knots	23,4 knots	95 men	CF Raúl Cao
ARA *Guerrico*	French A-69 Class Corvette	4.11.1978	1250 Tons	1-100/55 mm, 1-40/70 mm, 2-20mm, ASW 2 Mk32 torpedo tubes	4 Exocet MM38	P-32	4500 miles at 14 knots	23,4 knots	95 men	CF Carlos Alfonso
ARA *Granville*	French A-69 Class corvette	22.06.81	1250 Tons	1-100/55 mm, 1-40/70 mm, 2-20mm, ASW 2 Mk32 torpedo tubes	4 Exocet MM38	P-33	4500 miles at 14 knots	23,4 knots	95 men	CF Eduardo Pelayo

(Diagram by Author)

the Falklands/Malvinas to launch their air strikes and insert special forces. By doing so they had unknowingly entered the radius of action of the Argentine carrier's strike aircraft. This presented a unique opportunity for the Argentine fleet to carry out a surprise attack on the British capital units while they were distracted, engaged in other operations. But neither side knew the other's position.

The Argentines had four reconnaissance aircraft operating from the carrier ARA *25 de Mayo* as explorers. These old and fairly slow (120 knots) twin-engine Grumman S-2 Trackers were not designed for that task, and their crews were at great risk in each of these missions, but they had the help of a newly installed electronic countermeasures equipment that enabled detection of surface vessels at a distance of 70-90 miles.

The Argentine navy´s effort was crowned by success on 1 May, shortly after 15:30 when Lieutenant Commander Alberto Dabini´s S2F Tracker and his crew – flying below 1,000 feet, taunting British

Table 3: Task Forces (TFs) of the Argentine Navy, 30 April 1982		
Task Force	**Ship (hull number)**	**Commander**
TF.79.1	ARA *25 de Mayo* (V-2)	Captain José Sarcona
	ARA *Hercules* (D-1)	Commander Enrique Molina Pico
	ARA *Santisima Trinidad* (D-2)	Commander José Tejo
	SS *Campo Duran*	Captain Diego Gianca
TF.79.2	ARA *Drummond* (P-31)	Commander Raul Cao
	ARA *Guerrico* (P-32)	Commander Carlos Alfonso
	ARA *Granville* (P-33)	Commander Eduardo Pelayo
TF.79.3	ARA *General Belgrano* (C-4)	Captain Hector Bonzo
	ARA *Bouchard* (D-26)	Commander Washington Barcena
	ARA *Piedrabuena* (D-29)	Commander Horacio Grassi
	SS *Puerto Rosales*	Captain Radames Lupi

A-4Q Skyhawks on the flight deck of ARA *25 de Mayo* get ready to strike the British fleet. (Argentine Navy)

An A-4Q (serial 3-A-305) seen in process of preparation for anti-carrier strike on 1 May 1982. Visible in the foreground is a multiple ejector rack with three Mk.82 bombs, one of which had a 'personal message' for the Royal Navy. (Argentine Navy Photo)

surveillance – detected a group of enemy ships (one large and six medium) in a position 031 degrees to the north-northwest of the Falklands/Malvinas and about 100 miles from Port Stanley, that is, within the range of the Argentine carrier's strike aircraft. Rear Admiral Allara deduced that it must be the enemy fleet that was supporting the alleged British amphibious landing that had been reported to him minutes earlier. According to Vice Admiral Lombardo it was Rear Admiral Edgardo A. Otero who assured him from the islands that aircraft had been shot down and that there were British troops on the beach. This led him to signal Rear Admiral Allara: 'Enemy tide up, freedom of action'. In fact, it was a British diversion plan designed to measure the capacity of reaction and the magnitude of the Argentine forces in the islands.[37] Orders were issued immediately to prepare the A-4Q aircraft for launch with the morning twilight of 2 May.

Six A-4Q Skyhawk aircraft were each armed with four US-designed 250kg (500lbs) Mk.82 bombs with Mk.12 Snakeye retarding fins installed on a multiple ejector rack, while one aircraft was kept in reserve and as a tanker. The attack would be led by the CO Lieutenant Commander Rodolfo Castro Fox, who – despite being convalescent from a serious accident – insisted on leading his men. It was estimated that of the six aircraft, four would go on to drop their 500-pound bombs. The bewilderment and confusion of the enemy fleet would be exploited by the three small A-69 corvettes (ARA *Drummond*, ARA *Granville* and ARA *Guerrico*) – whose low silhouettes made them difficult to locate – to sneak upon the enemy and unleash their MM38s on enemy units scattered in the area or those that might be engaged in

An S-2E ASW Grumman Tracker landing on the carrier *25 de Mayo*. They had a range of 1,900 km and were used for anti-submarine and reconnaissance operations during the war. (Argentine Navy

Guided missile destroyer ARA *Hercules* sailing in the South Atlantic Ocean before the war. (Argentine Navy)

assisting the expected damaged target (one of the enemy aircraft carriers). At dusk, a second Tracker was launched in an attempt to update the enemy's position. Lieutenant Commander Emilio Goitia and his crew again located British ships about 60 miles southeast of the Argentine aircraft carrier. Goitia's escape proves that the British early warning and battle management were incomplete.

At about the same time and as a result of the sighting of the ARA *General Belgrano* and satellite help from US intelligence,[38] the British Battle Group Commander sent his own British Airspace Sea Harrier FR.Mk1 fighter jets into reconnaissance in a north-western direction, because he suspected being encircled by a classic pincer movement from different directions by multiple Argentine task forces. Correspondingly, Lieutenant Ian Mortimer was sent in that direction to investigate, with strict orders to fly in radar silence. He flew about 200 miles out and then descended to cover the next 40 miles at 200 feet. According to the pilot, 'There wasn't a sound from the radar warner and not a light to be seen anywhere.'[39]

Suspecting that his mission had been to no avail, he then decided to 'switch my radar to transmit and, as we expected it might, all hell broke loose! The next thing I knew I was being illuminated by all sorts of radar including Sea Dart fire-control, and I counted four ship contacts less than 25 miles away'.[40] There was only one thing left to do: turn off the radar and make a full-speed escape before a Sea Dart missile (from ARA *Hercules*) could shoot him down. The Blue Fox radar of Mortimer's Sea Harrier could not discriminate between types of ships but for the British it was a fair bet that if a Type 42 was there, then so was *25 de Mayo*.

Allara rightly believed that the location of ARA *25 de Mayo* was now compromised. The tactical surprise was lost. At dawn on 2 May, lack of wind on the flight deck prevented the jets from launching. The new configuration of the A-4Qs with a single 500-pound bomb only enabled a strike within an 80-mile range which made useless the cost-benefit of the operation. The 12-hour window he had had to attack had been lost.

Allara summed up what happened after the end of the conflict: 'The important thing about that morning, was that it was possible to verify that the British were not disembarking, and therefore their ships remained concentrated.'[41] Admiral Sandy Woodward confirms this conclusion in his personal diary where he wrote for Sunday 2

May: 'Nothing from the SSNs up north who should have intercepted *25 de Mayo* and her team. All in all, it seems the Args [*sic*] must have decided that we weren´t the landing force [they were expecting] after all, and that the sally wasn't worth the risk.'[42]

This passage reveals that the Argentine fleet sailed into harm's way, even in the presence of British SSNs already operating in the South Atlantic.

Finally, the above suggests that the Royal Navy Task Force actually refused to engage in combat with the Argentine fleet, after her whereabouts became known. Woodward instead led his ships well to the eastern limit of the Total Exclusion Zone, especially after 4 May. This defensive strategy confirms both his distrust in the Sea Harrier for anti-ship operations, and a major fear that one or both of the *25 de Mayo* escorts armed with Sea Dart missiles could strike a considerable blow to his rather thin aircraft wing.

Destroyer ARA *Bouchard*, one of the two escorts of the Belgrano, was armed with four Exocet MM38 launchers. (Argentine Navy)

ARA *Belgrano* sinking in the South Atlantic Ocean. Note the many life rafts drifting along the hull. (Argentine Navy)

The Sinking of the Cruiser Belgrano

The light cruiser ARA *General Belgrano* (Captain Hector Bonzo) patrolling between Staten Island and the Burdwood Bank, southwest of the Falklands/Malvinas, adopted a combat formation with her destroyers at the cruiser´s vanguard – separated 10,000 yards one from the other – anticipating an air threat from the Total Exclusion Zone.[43] Her mission was to prevent any British ships from joining the Royal Navy Task Force by approaching from the Pacific and intercept any surface units approaching the mainland from the south.[44]

Bonzo and his subordinate commanders erroneously thought that the priority targets for the enemy would be the destroyers ARA *Bouchard* (hull number D-26; Commander Washington Barcena) and ARA *Piedrabuena* (hull number D-29; Commander Horacio Grassi) both armed with Exocet MM38 missiles with a range of 40 miles. They were unaware that the British also assigned the Argentine cruiser the ability – which was inaccurate – to launch Exocets, which made it as 'priority' a target as the destroyers.

When finally, at 2:50 on 2 May, Allara´s signal was received cancelling the order to enter the Total Exclusion Zone towards the enemy, the cruiser changed course steering 270, now heading towards the mainland. Unfortunately, it did not alter the adopted formation (flexible stations). Among the different alternatives at his disposal, Bonzo could have chosen to place a destroyer screen on each side – given his low speed of just 10 knots – or simply increase speed and adopt a zig-zag pattern. These might have prevented him from being torpedoed as a sitting duck, as it would have substantially complicated the task of an enemy submarine. However, as none of this happened the fate of the cruiser was sealed.

At 16:01 (local time) on 2 May, the cruiser was hit by two old straight-running Mark 8 torpedoes (warhead of 363kg) of Second World War vintage, on its port side. The first struck the hull between the bow and the front 6-inch turret; the second exploded underneath the after superstructure, inside the engine room, leaving the vessel without propulsion and electrical power, with the rudder locked 15 degrees to port. Only 34 minutes later, the ship was listing so severely, that Bonzo was left without choice but to order his crew to abandon ship. The cruiser *Belgrano* thus became the first warship to be sunk by a nuclear attack submarine at war, leaving 323 dead, including three young midshipmen recently graduated from the Naval Academy.[45] At about the same time the destroyer ARA *Bouchard* felt what appeared to be a torpedo hit that failed to explode in her port quarter. As a result, both destroyers received orders to open distances between them and to search for the attacking

Cruiser ARA *General Belgrano* sinking after being hit by two Mk 8 torpedoes fired by HMS *Conqueror*. Note that the bow is missing. (Argentine Navy)

Photo of *Alférez Sobral* (A-9), an 800-tonne ocean-going tug. Acquired from the US Navy (where it served for the same purpose as USS *Salish*, ATA-187) in 1972, it served with the Argentine Navy until 2019. (Albert Grandolini Collection)

submarine. This naval action allowed sailors on both sides to come face to face with the true nature of naval warfare: fast, deadly and decisive.

The *Belgrano* could have had a different destiny had she not entered Ushuaia, where her presence was easily recognised by Chilean observers or informers. Moreover, at the time it was hit, the cruiser was in a straight line at just 10 knots on the grounds of having left behind the radius of action of the enemy´s naval aviation – without a screen of destroyers as an ASW defence. Thus, the chances of its crew preventing the *Conqueror* from launching its torpedoes at a distance of 1,500 yards – practically at point blank range – were almost nil. The subsequent analysis carried out by the Navy concluded that the cruiser had indeed made several doctrinal errors,[46] unlike their escorts whose commanders acted in accordance with the critical situation at hand. The sinking of the *Belgrano* demonstrated mainly that modern weapons are required to fight modern wars.

The tragic loss of this capital unit on 2 May 1982 produced a strong emotional impact on Admiral Anaya, accentuated soon afterwards by the ruthless attack on the 700-ton patrol boat ARA *Alferez Sobral* (hull number A-9; Lieutenant Commander Sergio Gomez Roca), which was engaged on a rescue mission. This led to the direct order given to Allara on 4 May to regroup his surface forces within shallow waters. Given the serious risk of losing the carrier, it was decided that the air wing should carry on fighting from bases on land, while the carrier returned to Puerto Belgrano.[47]

On this awkward position in which the navy found itself, Admiral Anaya reflected after the conflict:

> On May 3rd [*sic*] at 9:15 I sent a signal to the commander of the South Atlantic, with a copy to the Fleet Commander, to the Army C-in-C and the Air Force C-in-C saying:
>
> 'The enemy has access to satellite information on our surface fleet movements. It was suggested from Puerto Belgrano to disembark the A-4s so that they could continue operating from Rio Grande. I said that I concurred. Within the navy there were tremendous pressures put upon me to deploy the fleet, because they said it was a shame not to do so. Thus, I went to Puerto

Malvinas Naval Air Station. Second from the left Lt Cdr Marcelo Bóveda, the author's uncle, who was second in command of Logistics Squadron 51 that operated Lockheed Electra L-188 PF. (Argentine Naval Aviation Museum)

> Belgrano and told everyone that I was the only one responsible, and the only one who was going to be blamed for not deploying the fleet, except that someone presented me a plan that could destroy two British capital ships. If that could be achieved, I would offer the entire Argentine fleet.'[48]

'Having appreciated its inferiority' – says Wayne Hughes – 'the Argentine fleet did well to regroup its surface ships to territorial waters'.[49] This does not mean that the navy stopped fighting. Quite the contrary – as we shall see – it continued to do so without giving truce to the enemy through its highly professional naval aviation and the Marine Corps units deployed on the islands.

Fleet Air Arm Operations

The Argentine Naval Aviation (Comando de la Aviación Naval Argentina, COAN) was undoubtedly the subculture within the Navy that best adapted to the strategic challenge posed by the enemy and who best took advantage of the modern technology at their disposal. The high professionalism of this handful of fierce naval pilots was evident during the development of offensive actions, which were executed with great courage, outstanding skill and irrefutable determination, in conditions of extreme danger, causing damage to the enemy outside any proportion in relation to the means employed.

Naval aviators are neither better nor worse than others; they are different. No doubt the way they operate is unique from other pilots. Indeed, they are a unique brotherhood.

> It unites us – [said Captain Jorge Colombo[50]] – the fact of having to descend and then land on a small, slippery, corkscrewing flight-deck, which is most of the time elusive, almost moody. First you have to chase it and find it in the middle of the ocean. And not always on an aircraft carrier, because landing with a helicopter on a tiny flight deck that frequently pitches frightfully – like that of the destroyers, which are very small ships – is quite tricky. Have you any idea what it is like to land on a handkerchief above the deck of a destroyer, in the middle of the sea, without having any other place to go? That is perhaps what makes us different from the rest of the pilots, and equal among us.[51]

Ironically, the most important capital unit of the Argentine fleet, the aircraft carrier, could only operate with A-4Q Skyhawks, a single-seater fighter-bomber of American origin that constituted the only carrier air group wing, and the most lethal weapon – next to the Super Etendard that by then could operate only from land bases – in an eventual air battle with the enemy. As of 1982, COAN's remaining Skyhawks were all in a very bad shape, and when the crisis erupted, only one was operational. This suggests that Admiral Anaya was taking a huge gamble when he decided to escalate the conflict and jeopardise the fleet without having this essential component of the Argentine naval power fully ready for combat.

The Argentine Navy was the only one in Latin America with a long and rich tradition in the use of this type of combat platform, an experience that went back to 1958 with the acquisition of the light carrier ARA *Independencia*. It is well known that aircraft carriers provide ready-made air bases, almost from the moment they set sail. The use of the aircraft carrier – even one as old as the *25 de Mayo* – was the most efficient way to concentrate tactical aviation at sea with a view to its wide, flexible and even decisive employment in the conflict. As we shall see, naval aviators have a systematic, consistent and continuous training in operations against naval targets (a skill that air force pilots were lacking), which required, if necessary, to maximise their versatility.

But once the aircraft carrier was regrouped to shallow waters, it was necessary to extend the radius of action of the strike aircraft to about 930km to be able to reach the targets at sea. This was achieved thanks to the assistance of the only two Lokcheed KC-130 Hercules aircraft from the Argentine Air Force (Fuerza Aérea Argentina, FAA) whose magnificent crews displayed a high degree of professionalism, fulfilling their essential task throughout the conflict, supplying their own aircraft and those of the COAN. This is one of the very few examples where joint inter-service work at the tactical level paid off.

Continuous training with the Argentine Type 42 destroyers – which were identical to the enemy ships they would have to confront – allowed naval aviators to develop flight profiles to avoid their anti-aircraft defences and surprise the enemy, something that they repeatedly achieved without having to regret any losses, as in the case of the Super Etendards who managed to survive intact to the end of the conflict.

All naval pilots who served during the conflict were professionals and expert aviators; they knew perfectly well what they were doing and the perils to which they were exposed. The missions ordered by the naval high command were executed without measuring risks, with the final objective of destroying the Royal Navy Task Force, despite the fact that most of the time the aircraft were at the limit of their operational life and in marginal flying conditions. They all respected the traditional ethos of the Navy.

Many years after the conflict, Vice Admiral (Retired) Benito Rótolo – former A-4Q pilot and ex-Deputy Chief of the Navy – summed up the feelings of all naval aviators by saying:

> We did not have time to have any fear, everything happened in a fraction of a second, and it was seconds we had to attack, avoid being shot down and make a flush escape to return to base. We fought for the country and our flag, but even more so for the partner we had next to us. We were an appendix of an entire group of people that worked very hard to keep us flying and hoped that the material and our determination could come to the expected result. We never thought we could do it alone.[52]

The 3rd Naval Fighter-Bomber Squadron all together for the last time in Rio Grande Naval Base, on 20 May 1982. Lt Marquez (standing first on the left) was later shot down in San Carlos Water by a Sea Harrier. Lt. Cdr. Castro Fox, the squadron leader, is the third on the right (standing) beside him is Lt. Benito Rótolo, second from the right. (Espora Naval Aviation Museum, with permission)

A-4Qs on the Flight deck of ARA *25 de Mayo*. (Espora Naval Aviation Museum, with permission)

As of 1982, the COAN comprised three wings, each of which consisted of several squadrons operating specialised aircraft and helicopter types. Most of these were US-made and, because of an arms embargo imposed by Washington in 1978, short on spares and thus in poor condition. This was, amongst others, one of the reasons why the COAN then acquired Super Etendards from France, and the service thus ended operating these – organised into the 2nd Naval Fighter-Bomber Squadron (2da Escuadrilla Aeronaval de Caza y Ataque) – next to the surviving A-4Qs of the 3rd Naval Fighter-Bomber Squadron (3ra Escuadrilla Aeronaval de Caza y Ataque).

A-4Q Skyhawks

Orders to participate in Operation Azul/Rosario found the 3rd Squadron in a critical situation and with virtually with no operational aircraft. Persistent rumours among the officers and other ranks were that the unit would be disbanded due to the purchase of the brand new Super Etendard fighter bombers of French origin, which were equipped with the lethal Exocet AM39 missiles. All the squadron´s pilots had years of experience in this American single-seat jet and had developed together with the Mathematics Department of the National University of the South a unique combat doctrine in Latin America to attack naval targets in the open sea. The time had come to put the theory into practice.

COAN's Skyhawks were truly in poor condition as of 1982: most had exceeded the flying hours of their airframes, their cannons did not work, and rocket packs in their ejection seats had expired in December 1981. Nevertheless, ground crews were ordered to prepare them for operations, while five of the pilots qualified to fly them were immediately summoned to the headquarters. José Arca and Benito Rótolo returned from France where they were about to take the Super Etendard basic training course. Jorge *Mingo* Philippi, former squadron leader and then head of the Rio Grande Naval Air Base, volunteered to join the squadron on 11 April; others, such as Lieutenants Carlos Oliveira and Alejandro Olmedo returned to the squadron from other units.

The Skyhawk pilots were an elite group of naval officers. They were highly motivated and very professional. These men were able to land a jet at 250 knots in no more than 50 metres of runway – that was the distance available to land a Skyhawk on the flight deck of the aircraft carrier ARA *25 de Mayo* – 'but they must do it exactly on a very narrow yellow-painted strip, barely a metre wide to snag one of the six arresting lines. The margin of error is minimal, it almost

A-4Q ready to be launched in the carrier ARA *25 de Mayo* in 1980. (Espora Naval Aviation Museum, with permission)

does not exist!' recalled Lieutenant Commander Miguel Robles in an interview to *La Semana* magazine.[53] To achieve this highly professional level of flying many of them had flown the A-4Q for several years, frequently accumulating over 1,200 flight hours and more than 200 landings on the aircraft carrier.

The daily life of a fighter pilot of the 3rd Squadron – when on board an aircraft carrier – could be described as pure adrenaline, because although each take-off contained its share of risk, the most dramatic moment was always the landing. It is an extremely complex operation, where the pilot's expertise and that of a landing signals officer (LSO) located aft on the ship – both coordinated by the aircraft carrier control tower – come to play. The dangerous nature of carrier operations is given by the fact that the jets must descend in a very short space of the flight deck, but with their engines at full power and enough fuel to take-off again if any factor prevents the pilot from snagging one of arresting wires spanned across the landing deck. Under these conditions, the possibility of an emergency – with its fire sequel on the flight deck – is always latent. Everything happens in a few seconds and develops more or less as follows. Once the pilot requests permission to land on the flight deck – of scarce 200 metres – all personnel completely clear the deck and all firemen get ready, including a powerful tractor that – in extreme cases – will push the wrecked aircraft into the sea to prevent the fire spreading on the flight deck or other aircraft. Simultaneously, two Alouette rescue helicopters are launched: one will remain on board and the other will hover over the carrier on her starboard quarter, a hundred metres high.

On the stern in the landing area, six arrestor wires tensioned transversely two metres apart are arranged for the A-4s to hook on them when landing. Everything is ready. When the pilot is authorised to land, another one – located at the far end of the stern – begins issuing the first instructions by radio: he is the LSO, an expert naval aviator who, in addition to being a very skilled pilot, can only carry out that delicate mission after having witnessed no fewer than a thousand landings on aircraft carriers. When the aircraft is already a few metres from the flight deck, a landing system using different lights, commanded from the control tower, is responsible for complementing the LSO's task. The sequence of lights indicates to the pilot the necessary corrections for a safe landing. If all goes well, the tail hook will catch one of the six arrest wires on deck and the aircraft will violently decelerate from about 100 to 0 knots in less than three seconds. Only when the pilot feels he has caught one of the arrest wires does he cut the power of the engines and stop the jet on its tracks. The complete manoeuvre lasts just 60 seconds, enough to mount a kind of synchronised show – deafening, always exciting and also, always impregnated with an unusual drama: in this everyday scene performed on the high seas, there is always a pilot whose life is at stake; none of the 200 men who are directly involved in the operation, minimise the drama that stains each landing.[54]

Working feverishly, by 29 March, ground crews of the 3rd Naval Fighter-Bomber Squadron made Skyhawks operational, and these were promptly deployed on board ARA *25 de Mayo* to assist in the Falklands/Malvinas landings. Meanwhile, the rest of the aircraft underwent an urgent refit programme to extend their operational life so that by 18 April, eight A-4Q jets and 12 pilots were integrated into the carrier air group. Between 18 April and 9 May the squadron operated from the aircraft carrier but without engaging in any combat actions.

On 14 May, the unit was re-deployed to the Naval Air Base Admiral Quijada in Rio Grande, awaiting the occasion of its baptism by fire. The squadron leader, Lieutenant Commander Rodolfo Castro Fox – still recovering from serious injuries received in an aircraft crash – organised the squadron into two sections of three aircraft each, in a bomber configuration, keeping one Skyhawk in reserve and another configured as a tanker. The 12 pilots were distributed in four groups of three members each, under the command of four

Skyhawk A-4Qs on the flight deck of ARA *25 de Mayo* during an exercise in 1980. (Author's private collection)

Lt Cdr Alberto Philippi and Lt José Arca pose for the camera just before the take-off. (Photo by Alberto Phillipi)

veteran pilot officers. The average age of the pilots was about 29-30 years. At that time, they had great skill and good technical and tactical preparation against naval targets.

The first combat mission was carried out on 21 May against British surface units operating in San Carlos Water. The strike was carried out by two sections of three A-4Q Skyhawks each. The first section was led by Lieutenant Commander Alberto Philippi, Lieutenant José Arca and First Lieutenant Commander Marcelo Marquez. Each carried four Snakeye Mk.82 bombs but not all had fully operational navigational equipment, and none was equipped with radar warning receivers that would alert their pilots if they were being illuminated by an enemy radar.

Once airborne and underway to the combat zone, the A-4Qs had to fly at an altitude of 30,000ft (9,144m) to save fuel before descending to only 100ft (30m) for the last leg of 100 miles to the islands. Like most Argentine fighter-bomber formations in those days, they entered the combat zone through the southern end of San Carlos Water, all the time flying through low clouds and rain, even if descending to only 50ft (15m) above the waves. The two sections were about 10 minutes apart. Due to some operational misunderstanding, the Grumman Tracker S-2E aircraft that had to provide them with information about the targets, could not contact them before the attack.

The first target that appeared that morning was the Type 21 frigate HMS *Ardent* (F-184; Commander Alan West) that was located south of the Ruiz Puente bay, in the middle of San Carlos. The first section achieved at least two hits on the stern deck of the ship; one of the bombs hit the hangar, blowing the Seacat launcher into the air, which seconds later crashed down on the flight deck killing the supply officer, the Lynx pilot and other crew members.[55] This enabled the second section (Lieutenant Benito Rótolo, Lieutenant Roberto Silvester and Lieutenant Carlos Lecour) that appeared minutes later, to drop their bombs without any interference, but this momentous event remained unknown to the Argentine pilots at the time of the attack, as Vice Admiral (retired) Benito Rótolo later recalled when describing his unprecedented experience:

> Once we passed the coastline, flying at low level over the sound, we realised that there were warships lying close to the coast. It was a peculiar day with squalls, sun, rain, and some clearings in the sky. The enemy ships opened up on us with everything they had during our approach, which was perpendicular to the target, in the centre of the sound. The Type 21 frigate [HMS *Ardent*] began to shoot at us with small arms fire as well as the other units. We could see all the shell splashes on the water. To evade the defensive fire, we made the classic zig-zag manoeuvre…not a very effective defence, but it was the only thing we could do given the circumstances…and it worked, because we were not hit. In addition, we expected to be engaged by Seacat missiles, but they didn't show up …[56]

During the second strike the frigate received more bomb hits in the stern section, one of which embedded itself underneath its fuel tanks, very close to the starboard quarter, wrapping the ship in a black cloud of smoke and splinters, which subsequently generated a large fire. As the conflagration rapidly went out of control, Commander West lost all communications and steering. The ship was taking lots of ice-cold sea water through a hole on the water line: essentially, *Ardent* was sinking. Most of the wounded – 37 men – and dead – 22 men – belonged to the damage control teams which were fighting the fire in the hangar.[57]

In the subsequent escape the first section was intercepted by a combat air patrol of two Sea Harriers, that shot down Lieutenant Commander Philippi with a Sidewinder missile, and with 30mm cannons caused the explosion in mid-air of First Lieutenant Commander Marcelo Marquez's aircraft. Lieutenant Arca's A-4 was also seriously damaged. The section leader Philippi managed to eject, descending under a parachute into the ice-cold waters of the sound. However, the pilot managed to swim to the coast and

A-4Q (3-A-307) getting ready to be launched from ARA 25 de Mayo during 1980. (Author's private collection)

was infectious, and conductive to heightened morale', wrote Svendsen after the war.[58]

After the conflict, Captain (Retired) Roberto Sylvester, a former A-4Q pilot, reflected on his participation in the conflict:

> I learned during the Falklands/Malvinas War that in critical situations our strength often comes from outside … and that true synergy is based on the sum of small things that day after day, man after man, weakness after strength, strength after weakness, solidify the unity, the attitude and the willingness of the group as a whole …[59]

Captain (now Lt Coronel retired) Jorge Svendsen with the author in Campo de Mayo around 2007. (Authors collection)

survived for four days on West Falkland until he was eventually rescued. Lieutenant Arca – although badly injured – managed to reach Port Stanley where he ejected into the sea near Port Stanley, as his aircraft was in no condition for a landing attempt. A Bell UH-1H helicopter pilot of the Argentine Army (Captain Jorge Svendsen) literally had to fish him from the sea – by sinking a ski in the water – as his chopper did not have any rescue equipment. The second section returned without incident to its base in Rio Grande, with some splinter impacts on its aircrafts' fuselages.

That same night Captain Svendsen attended with his crew to visit Arca at the local hospital with the idea that they were going to find a dejected man, with no more desire to fight and eager to return home. Great was his surprise when, 'I heard Lieutenant Arca say that his only concern was to return to the mainland to get a new aircraft so that he could carry on fighting the British. His fighting spirit

In eight days of operations the A-4Qs completed 29 missions during which 43 Mk.82 bombs with Mk.12 Snakeye retarding fins were deployed and 662 rounds fired from 20mm cannons. The squadron suffered the loss of two pilots (First Lieutenant Commander Marcelo Marquez and Lieutenant Commander Carlos Zubizarreta) and three aircraft. In turn, the 3rd Naval Fighter-Bomber Squadron was responsible for the sinking of the Type 21 frigate HMS *Ardent* and damage of various extents to other warships of the task force. The squadron was withdrawn to its home base at Espora Naval Base on 20 June 1982, earning the Battle Honours: *Honor al valor en combate*.[60]

Super Etendard

The 2nd Naval Fighter-Bomber Squadron under the command of Commander Jorge Colombo – which had just five aircraft – had an impact early on with the sinking of the HMS *Sheffield*. The attack left 20 dead and 24 wounded. This mission was carried out on 4 May with a section of two Super Etendards (Lieutenant Commander Augusto Bedacarratz and Lieutenant Armando Mayora) in broad daylight. Although one out of two AM39 Exocets released at this opportunity missed its target, the other proved sufficient to knock out its target.

The Super Etendards had been vectored to the target thanks to the help of an old Lockheed P-2 Neptune maritime patrol aircraft (serial 2-P-112; commanded by Lieutenant Commander Ernesto Proni Leston), that was at the limit of its operational life and with its electronic equipment very degraded. In order to maintain the exploration and permanently update the position of the targets, they had to remain in flight for seven hours – a record for an aircraft manufactured back in the 1950s. Working on basis of crystal technology and suffering from old vacuum tubes that frequently burned out (so much so, that their operators always carried spares in their pockets), it failed several times during the mission. Nevertheless, the Neptune served its purpose by establishing that at least four targets – one of them 'large' – were underway around 85 miles south of Port Stanley (and about 90 miles from the 2-P-112). Proni Leston would remember after the conflict: 'Our plane did not fly on fuel; it flew on a wing and a prayer.'[61]

Lieutenant Ian Inskip – then navigator of the destroyer HMS *Glamorgan* – reveals what has come to be called *the Sheffield*

The Neptune was the oldest aircraft in the Navy's inventory. It had a range of 4,600 km and a speed of 555km/h. One of these aircraft was responsible for detecting the British surface force on picket duty that ended with the strike and subsequent loss of HMS *Sheffield*. (Argentine Navy)

syndrome, that took over the British fleet from that day on and would not leave them until the end of the conflict:

> At 14:20, *Sheffield* [Capt Sam Salt] on picket duty, reported she was on fire with a 15 ft hole in her side. She was 12 miles from us and I could see a cloud of yellowish smoke rising amidships ... *Arrow* and *Yarmouth* were dispatched to assist and at the same time *Glasgow* reported seeing a periscope. I recorded, "We are under attack but we do not know what from ... everyone is very jumpy!" *Glasgow* launched a torpedo at the submarine ... An updated report indicated that *Sheffield* had suffered an underwater explosion close to the ops room ... At 15:28 Arrow reported a torpedo to the north. *Sheffield*, now twenty miles from us, was billowing smoke which started to blacken as the fires worsened. This was not a good sign ... *Yarmouth* reported a torpedo and attacked with mortar whilst *Glasgow* gained sonar contact. Reports of torpedoes continued unabated and my narrative observed, "won´t they be using electric torpedoes that leave no trail?"[62]

Ironically, *Sheffield* – intended to alert the British fleet to enemy air raids – was not on full alert at the time of the attack: its ops room failed to pick up the Argentine aircraft approaching. Her CO, Captain Sam Salt, was in his day cabin, and her chaff was not launched. In addition, its aluminium hull was not sufficient to receive damage, and ultimately the ship was lost by a large fire on board. The days when a warship could receive several impacts and continue fighting had passed. Warheads of modern weapons were much more lethal.

After the conflict the British claimed that one of the Exocet missiles had not hit the target and that the second had hit *Sheffield* without detonating, although causing the fire that ultimately ended with the ship sinking. Captain Colombo has his own idea of what could have happened. He admits that:

> As far as I am concerned both missiles hit the target and detonated. Taking into account the conditions in which they were launched [from the same point and almost simultaneously] and also what Sheffield´s captain, Sam Salt, initially declared [he confessed to the BBC that he had heard two explosions] I have no doubt that the two hit, that maybe they entered through the same hole and that the two hit or at least one of them.[63]

The official report of the British Ministry of Defence indicates the moment of impact at 14:03 at the level of the second deck on the starboard side, a few feet above the waterline, between the auxiliary machinery space and the forward engine room. The missile had opened a hole in her side of 15ft by 4ft. The report concluded with: 'The evidence suggests that the warhead did not detonate. There are few reports of shrapnel. Large fires spread ... the acrid black smoke quickly spread through the central section of the ship and up to the bridge ... the fuel from the missile and diesel ...were the main source of this smoke.'[64]

The French questioned the equivocal diagnosis of the British by pointing out that:

> The *Sheffield* was hit by an Argentine Exocet twenty years after the first rumours that the missile did not work. The defenders of that thesis point out that the *Sheffield* was not destroyed by the missile, contrary to what happened with target ships used during mock attacks in peace time. A difference that is explained by the *Sheffield*'s modular construction design. The first newspaper articles indicated that the missile had detonated, but soon other columnists began to question the value of the Exocet. According to them, the fuel that had not been consumed in the missile's body caused the fire that proved fatal to the *Sheffield*.[65]

This hypothesis seems difficult to sustain, since the missile was launched at the limit of its range and therefore there would be very little residual fuel left in its tank. Although experts recognise that – in exceptional circumstances – the missile's warhead may not detonate, evidence suggests that the missile that hit *Sheffield* worked normally. The steel plates of the hull at the point of impact were broken outwards, which proves that an explosion took place inside. Moreover, if the missile had not exploded, it would most likely have crossed the ship from side to side, as happened with many Argentine bombs several times. This rumour – encouraged by industrial competitors for understandable reasons – was also encouraged by British naval officers.[66]

The unexpected sinking of HMS *Sheffield* caused a huge psychological impact on the enemy's task force and a devastating blow to the British government. This is reflected by Commander Chris Craig, Commanding Officer of the Type 21 frigate *Alacrity*, who stated in his memoirs after the war: 'Despite the importance of Chris Wreford-Brown´s [*Conqueror´s* skipper] achievement, *Sheffield* was planted deep in the subconscious; and the invincibility of the Royal Navy had been too readily dispelled.'[67] Well-known British journalist and historian Simon Jenkins stated years later in an interview with an Argentine newspaper: 'The sinking of the *Sheffield* ... was the worst moment of the war. That's when the government thought it could not win the war'.[68]

When the British Commander-in-Chief Fleet sent his report to the Undersecretary of the Navy on 13 September 1982, he commented: '[*Sheffield*] was carried away by a false sense of security

Super Etendards at Espora Naval Air Base at the end of 1982. (Espora Naval Aviation Museum, with permission)

in the face of the inefficiency of previous Argentine air raids. Her loss was a clear warning and a foretaste of the true ability of the Argentines'.[69]

Lt. Julio "Mate" Barraza returns to Rio Grande after his successful mission against *Atlantic Conveyor*. (Espora Naval Aviation Museum, with permission)

The Loss of SS *Atlantic Conveyor*

During the days, and then weeks following the attack on HMS *Sheffield* the conditions were much less favourable for the Argentine Naval Aviation. The Royal Navy Task Force was now on her guard and the Argentine Navy no longer had any maritime reconnaissance aircraft available. Fortunately, Port Stanley´s radar – although it could not detect ships beyond the horizon – could very well follow the flights of Sea Harriers and helicopters up to a distance of 100 miles from the archipelago. Its operators had noticed that enemy air traffic always appeared and disappeared at the same points. There was no doubt, then, that the enemy aircraft carriers continued to operate from the same positions.

This tactical error was going to prove fatal for the 18,000-ton Cunard Line's SS *Atlantic Conveyor* (Captain Ian North) that lacked any individual defence. This container ship – hastily turned into an auxiliary aircraft transport – had embarked at Ascension Island eight Sea Harriers and six British Aerospace Harrier GR.Mk 3 attack jets, five Boeing CH-47 Chinooks and eight Westland Wessex H.Mk V transport helicopters. She was loaded to the gunwales with stores and ammunition including 600 cluster bombs for the Harriers and all the equipment needed to construct an airstrip for Harriers in the beachhead area in San Carlos Water. The Harriers were quickly flown off as soon as *Conveyor* reached the Battle Group on 19 May: however, helicopters remained on board, for the British planned to use them to speed-up the advance of their ground troops.

SS *Atlantic Conveyor* was scheduled to enter San Carlos Water on the night of 25-26 May to unload in the dark hours her priceless helicopters. It was therefore a target of capital importance, since its loss – with all the aforementioned equipment – would have serious consequences in the development of British ground operations.

The Argentine pilots considered the *Atlantic Conveyor* an 'aircraft carrier'. Still, they ignored which of the positions reported by Port Stanley corresponded respectively to *Invincible*, *Hermes* or the converted merchant. All they knew was that in each of the positions reported there was a possible aircraft carrier and that if there were many vessels at the indicated point, that type of capital ship should surely be the one that produced the strongest radar signal. The Super Etendards could not approach the target directly from the west, because in that case they would have presented themselves just where the British expected them to appear. Instead, the strike against the *Atlantic Conveyor* was carried out from the northeast, following a long detour more than 100 miles north of the Falklands/

Malvinas, which made multiple in-flight refuellings necessary on the way in and out.

The enemy task force had been forced to come in closer than before because of the need to support the landing force under air attack at San Carlos. Lieutenant Commander Roberto Curilovic and Lieutenant Julio Barraza took off in mid-afternoon. In a perfectly executed operation, the two Super Etendards were refuelled twice and then approached the task force from the north. They detected the British ships at their first attempt, launched their Exocets and turned for home. The strike had come closer to hitting an aircraft carrier than they knew. The task force was always deployed in such a way that other ships were positioned between the vital aircraft carriers and the likely approach of Exocets. *Atlantic Conveyor* was in the last row of these protective screen of ships and if she had not attracted the missiles, one or another of Exocets might have run on into the aircraft carrier area.

A freighter is much less compartmentalised, has fewer firefighting devices and fewer damage control personnel on board than a warship. With the simultaneous impact of two Exocets on the port quarter – 10 feet above the waterline – below the superstructure and on the aft cargo deck, the ship and her particularly flammable helicopter cargo, including thousands of ammunition boxes and fuel barrels, had no chance of survival. *Atlantic Conveyor* quickly fell prey to the flames: the generators fell out first, stopping the fire mains and thus dooming the precious ship. Not only her skipper, Captain Ian North (twice sunk during the Second World War, and posthumously awarded the Distinguished Service Cross), but also 12 other men perished.

The Strike on HMS *Invincible*

The last Etendard–Exocet strike was carried out on 30 May. Although only one missile was left by the time, two Super Etendards – crewed by Lieutenant Commander Alejandro Francisco and Lieutenant Luis Collavino – and four Skyhawk aircraft of the Air Force (piloted by 1st Lieutenant Omar Castillo, 1st Lieutenant José Vazquez, 1st Lieutenant Ernesto Ureta and Lieutenant Gerardo Isaac) were involved. This time, the target was the HMS *Invincible*, whose position was plotted to about 100 miles south-east of Port Stanley. Correspondingly, the approach took place from south-east this time, as the only possibility of achieving surprise. Obviously, this represented a major detour, even longer than that given for the previous attack.

Once again, the missile was launched from a distance that assured the impact and in excellent conditions, with on-screen radar echo, also confirmed by the second Super Etendard. The A-4s then followed the Exocet towards the target. Two were shot down by Royal Navy`s Type 42 destroyer HMS *Exeter* (hull number D-89), but the other two attacked and subsequently declared that they had seen a column of smoke rising from the middle of a ship they identified as HMS *Invincible*. The British deny that this ever happened, and stress that the warship attacked by the two surviving Skyhawks was the frigate HMS *Avenger* (F-185), which – together with *Exeter* – was south-east of the Royal Navy Task Force. To this day, Argentine and other Spanish-language analysts debate whether the HMS *Invincible* was damaged – or not.[70]

As a result of the attacks on *Sheffield* and *Atlantic Conveyor*, the Royal Navy aircraft carriers had to stay well away to the east of the Falklands/Malvinas, since the operational benefits of the proximity were totally distorted by the greater share of risk faced. This had a great impact on British airborne operations, as it forced the Combat Air Patrols to make a 180-mile transit to the area of operations and have only 20 minutes to remain on station before having to return to the aircraft carrier with a minimum of fuel. This modality significantly reduced the Harriers' chances of beating Argentine aircraft over the Falklands/Malvinas.

The outstanding performance of the Argentine pilots deserved the following reflection by famous French ace of the Second World War Pierre Clostermann: 'Never in the history of wars since 1944, did airmen have to face such a terrifying conjunction of mortal obstacles, nor even those of the RAF over London in 1940 or those of the Luftwaffe in 1945 … The truth is only validated when blood is spilled… the world believes only in causes whose witnesses are killed by it.'[71]

Submarine Warfare

As described above, submarines were clearly a secondary element in the institutional culture of the Argentine Navy of 1982, in spite that these combat platforms representing the best way to neutralise the Royal Navy during the conflict. Unfortunately, in the period 1933-1982 the few submarines available were used mainly as targets for the fleet´s surface ships and not in drills against surface combatants. For this purpose, it was sufficient for the boats to maintain the ability to submerge – and then only during the time necessary for the exercises.[72]

As a result of this erratic policy and the high cost of the SST-4 wire guided torpedoes no mock attacks were conducted before the conflict or at the beginning of April with real live combat warheads. Exercise torpedoes were used instead with their warheads full of sea water. Thus, a generation of submariners grew up without ever

Submarine ARA *Santa Fe* (S-21) returning to Mar del Plata Naval Base in 1978. (Argentine Navy)

Submarine ARA *San Luis* (S-32) sailing on the surface near her home base at Mar del Plata. (Argentine Navy)

having seen or heard a torpedo explode. This lack of realism in the peacetime exercises had a serious consequence: the design defects that the new SST-4 torpedoes had remained invisible to the Navy.

This was not an obstacle for Argentine submariners to stand out during the exercises carried out with friendly navies in peacetime, as evidenced by the 1981 UNITAS exercise where the Argentine Navy participated alongside naval units of the US Navy. Admiral USN Thomas Hayward – Chief of Naval Operations at the time – was informed of the high marks obtained by Argentine submariners during the aforementioned exercise and this was later transmitted to his British allies.

In this context, 2 April surprised the Argentine submarine force with just four boats in service – two of them of the old vintage US Guppy-class – ARA *Santa Fe* (Commander Horacio Bicain) and ARA *Santiago del Estero* (Lieutenant Commander Hector Perez) – both at the end of their operational life – and two modern, German built 209-class: ARA *Salta* (Commander Manuel Riveiro –Commander Roberto Salinas) and ARA *San Luis* (Commander Fernando Azcueta). ARA *Santiago del Estero* (ex-USS *Chivo*) had been decommissioned in September 1981. To conceal this from the enemy she was ordered to sail surreptitiously on the surface under her own power to Puerto Belgrano Naval Base where it remained hidden during the rest of the conflict, making the enemy believe that it was operational.

ARA *Santa Fe* – ex-USS *Catfish* – made two war patrols, despite having her operational capabilities considerably reduced. In particular, her sensors were unreliable and her batteries could take only a limited charge. In spite of this, she managed to elude the narrow blockade imposed by the enemy around South Georgia – which included the presence of the nuclear attack submarine HMS *Conqueror* – and disembark cargo and support personnel. This unit was lost on 26 April when it was unable to avoid an attack by enemy helicopters, being subsequently sunk by its crew in Grytviken, South Georgia.[73]

Of the two 209-class, ARA *Salta* (S-31) made excessive noise on her trials that prevented her deployment to the area of operations.[74] Only ARA *San Luis* (S-32) was technically fully operational, and all the hopes rested solely on her performance. However, from the beginning of her patrol, the fire control computer broke down,

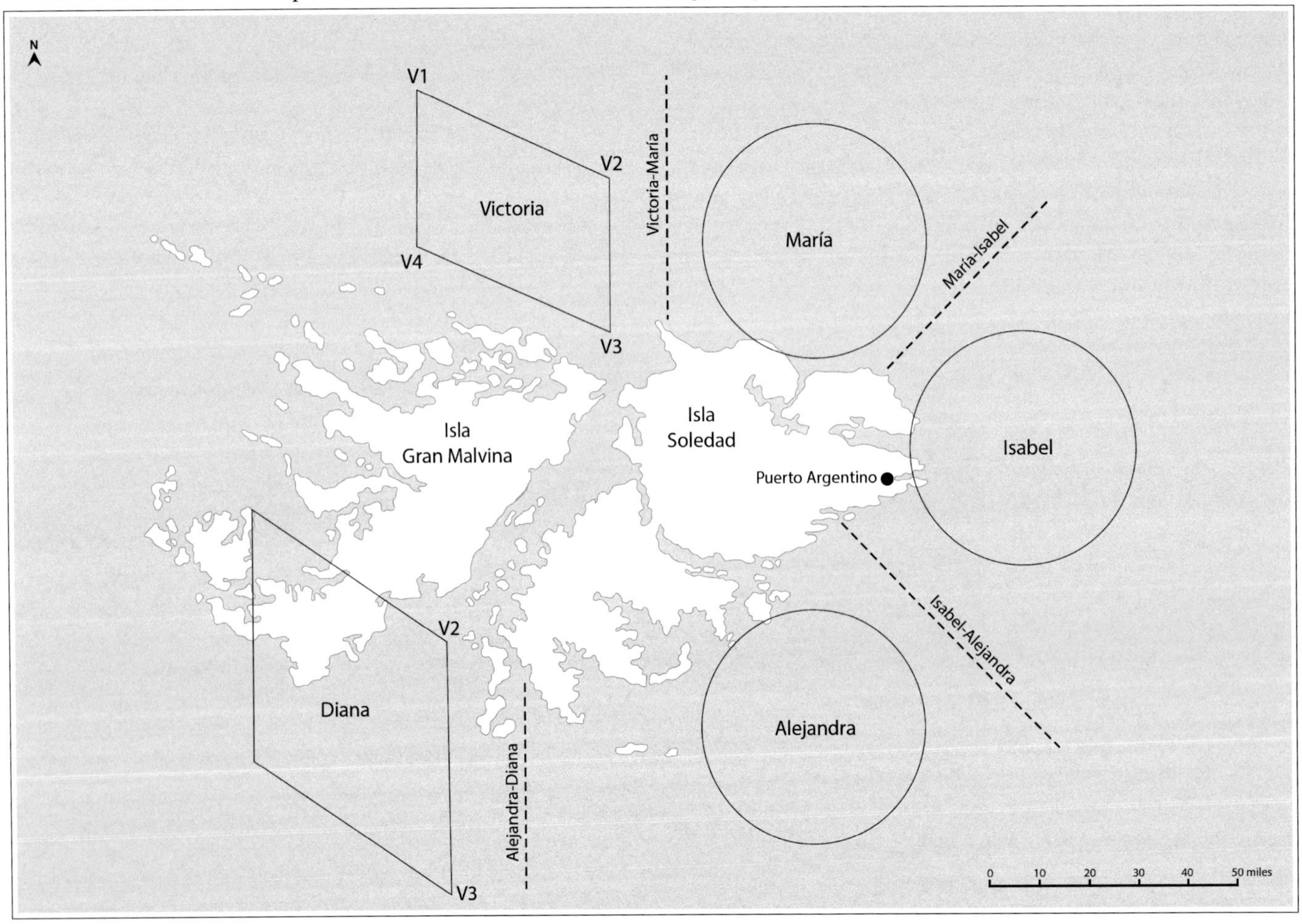

Operational areas of Argentine Navy's submarines around the Falkland/Malvinas Islands during the war of 1982. (Map by George Anderson)

Santa Fe moored at the British Antarctic Survey Pier at Grytviken after being captured. (Guy Sheridan)

ARA *Santa Fe* was scuttled by her crew and rested at the bottom of the harbour. (Guy Sheridan)

ARA *Santa Fe* (S-21) after her capture by the British in King Edward Cove. (Guy Sheridan)

ARA *Santa Fe* at Grytviken after her capture by the British. (Guy Sheridan)

forcing the crew to use it in the emergency mode; this meant manually. Despite all these setbacks Commander Azcueta managed to attack two surface targets and a suspected enemy submarine. The first two torpedoes failed to hit the target because the wire guide broke after two to three minutes of running and the third one – although it did detonate – it was not possible to find out if it had hit the target. After the war the enemy only recognised that one of its conventional submarines had been damaged by colliding against the bottom.[75]

The gallant performance of ARA *San Luis* in conditions of extreme adversity against an overwhelming enemy that specialised in ASW is a clear example of the high quality of the Argentine submarine crews. This outstanding performance facing the entire British Task Force single-handed was comparable with the best of Argentina´s naval traditions. Had the Argentine submariners been able to sink a few key naval units, the British would have been faced with a longer and increasingly more difficult task. But with only one modern submarine available, the odds were against them. However, the expert British naval forces – which at the time carried out nearly 70 percent of the Atlantic

Alliance's anti-submarine patrols – received this unexpected lesson from a single conventional submarine which they were – ultimately – powerless to neutralise.

The Marine Corps

The Marine Corps was another of the Argentine Navy subcultures that was put to the test during the conflict. This elite regiment was integrated with the infantry units of the Argentine Army and was deployed in the hills around Port Stanley. However, the Argentine commanders realised how isolated and unsupported their positions were. General Menéndez was urging them to be more aggressive, but the whole build-up and dispositions of the land forces around the Stanley area had been based on an agreed policy of static defence.

The strength of the Argentine units was between 8,500 and 9,000 men – composed of six infantry units, five Army regiments and a Marine infantry battalion – to face the seven British infantry battalions that would take part in the battle. The Argentines had 45 field guns – three of 155 mm and 42 of 105 mm – which were stocked with at least 10,000 rounds of ammunition. The British had just thirty 105 mm guns but counted with the advantage of naval gunfire support from ships operating each night off the coast.[76]

The 5th Marine Infantry Battalion (BIM 5) under Commander Carlos Robacio had a well-balanced set of weapons and excellent communications equipment. But much more important was that he had men who – as a result of the Navy's conscript system – resulted in the unit having a much higher level of training than the Army, and there were none of the younger 1963 class recruits present. His men adapted well to the terrain and extreme weather conditions, as their natural base was in Rio Grande, Tierra del Fuego.

Another important advantage was that it was supported by its own Marine Artillery Battery and had its own logistics system that supplied it with its own naval air transports from the mainland, managing to maintain excellent combat skills.

The Marine battalion´s sector of responsibility included the heights of Mount Tumbledown, Mount William and Sapper Hill, located 7.6km and 2.5km west and southeast of Port Stanley respectively. The Battalion Headquarters was situated one and a half miles behind Tumbledown, nearly halfway back to Stanley.

The late Rear Admiral (retired) Robacio disagreed with the general defence dispositions adopted by the Army but was powerless to convince Menéndez that he was wrong. After the war he recalled:

Since the available intelligence provided a priority for an amphibious assault on the Port Stanley area, the defence dispositions adopted were exclusively for this purpose. The Army High Command on the islands stayed convinced and clinging to that idea, although we advised that the most logical move was an enemy landing without opposition in the west.[77]

Subsequent events proved that Robacio was right when the British finally landed in San Carlos Water on 21 May.

The Scots Guards were the British unit in charge of taking Mount Tumbledown. This rocky ridge – a mile and a half long but very narrow, 750 feet high at its most prominent point – completely dominated a large area of open ground and was certainly the key point in the remaining defences around Stanley. The British plan for the main attack was to tackle the ridge in three phases, working from west to east, with each of the battalion´s three rifle companies capturing in turn approximately one-third of the objective.[78]

Lieutenant Eduardo Villarraza´s Nacar Company was the only one present to defend Tumbledown. This was a strong company, with four instead of the normal three Marine platoons, plus a Marine engineer platoon and about 50 men from Army units. This unit was particularly well supported by mortar and heavy machine gun detachments. But nearly all of the company was on the eastern end of the ridge, deployed to dominate the open ground to the north and the south, where the main British attack was expected. This left Sub Lieutenant Carlos Vazquez´s No.4 Platoon to face the Scots Guards in the middle of the ridge single-handed. Eventually this unit became known as *the heroes of Tumbledown*. These men held up the Scots Guards for many hours, killing five guardsmen and wounding 30 others. Of the 26 marines in Vazquez´s platoon six were killed and four wounded, while the Army personnel suffered more than 50 percent casualties, including 2nd Lt Silva and several wounded. This combined Marine/Army platoon thus suffered more than 50 percent casualties.[79]

An eyewitness account from a British war correspondent describes the Argentine Marines in action:

> The Scots Guards could hear some of the Argentines shouting and even singing as they fought. These were the best troops General Menéndez could put into the field, the 5th Marines, ninety-two strong, supported by mortars and ten sustained fire machine guns. As the night wore on and the fierce firefight continued, they showed no sign of crumbling, and their main positions held firm … The Guards reached the last of the enemy positions on Tumbledown only after a further six hours of struggle inch by inch up the rocks … The battalion had lost a total of nine men

ARA *Cabo San Antonio*, one of two amphibious assault ships that played a crucial role by deploying the Argentine Marines during the invasion of the Falklands/Malvinas on 2 April 1982. (Albert Grandolini Collection)

killed and 43 wounded to capture one of the most strongly defended Argentine positions of the war.[80]

Given the unfavourable evolution of the situation around 7 in the morning on 14 June, the BIM 5 was ordered to retreat. Robacio explains why he did not agree:

> I was convinced that we could still resist, so *O company* – which had already recovered – was ordered to get ready for a joint counterattack with *M company*, an attack that I planned to direct personally. As time went by, the situation from the logistical point of view became critical, given that the ammunition of the support weapons – 105mm shells of our battery, mortars and anti-tank guns – had practically run out. We had not received the required ammunition reinforcement and only received 81mm mortar ammunition from the rear, in a vehicle that reached the Engineers HQ (8-9 km from the front line). The action of the enemy artillery was terrible.[81]

Around noon on 14 June, the Argentine Military High Command ordered the surrender on the islands. The armed struggle for the Falkland/Malvinas Islands was over. The attackers said they had nine dead and 41 wounded. When the men of BIM 5 marched to captivity, Lieutenant Colonel Vaux – commander of the 42nd Marine Commando – drew attention to the fact that 'The brave enemies of Mount Tumbledown marched martially and carried up the banners of the unit along the streets of Port Stanley'.[82]

From the testimonies collected it can be concluded that BIM 5 demonstrated a high degree of readiness, and great professionalism in the execution of the defence of Port Stanley. The unit lost in combat 17 men (two NCOs and 15 conscripts).

The Navy's Weapons Engineers

There are numerous situations in which the Argentinians, in the absence of adequate means, were forced to improvise. This is one such case. The Argentine forces on the Falklands/Malvinas were confronted with a very serious problem: how to neutralise the enemy´s naval gunfire support, which constantly bombed the Argentine positions from the sea without being molested. The senior naval officer on the islands pursued an alternative strategy which was intended to make use of the Exocet´s lethal firepower in a way which no one – least of all the Royal Navy – could have anticipated.

Towards the end of May Rear Admiral Edgardo Otero – the senior naval officer in Port Stanley – urged the naval staff on the mainland to find some kind of defence against these attacks. Rear Admiral Gualter Allara conceived the idea of using the surface-launched Exocet MM38 launchers mounted normally on warships as a coastal battery. As it has happened countless times, in all armed conflicts the question was not what had to be done, but how to do it. Until then there was no such system in use in the world market, but that did not stop the weapons engineers of the Argentine Navy.

Commander Julio Pérez (later Rear Admiral), was ordered by Allara to study the feasibility of dismantling the installation of Exocet missiles from any ship and take it to the Falklands/Malvinas as a coastal battery. Pérez answered that such a task would require no less than 45 days and that the system would be very difficult to move. Allara told him they did not have that time. Faced with the seriousness of the situation, Pérez said that he would try to improvise something faster that would adapt to the navy´s needs.

Pérez was a brilliant weapons engineer who had spent just 10 months in Paris studying the complexities of the Exocet but did not underestimate the task ahead of him. By this time, he had already managed to master the art of linking the AM39 missile to the Super Etendard, even though he had only minimal experience with this sophisticated equipment. What should I say were the qualities of this splendid officer? Noble mindedness. An even temperament. Sensitivity. Determination. A lively mind. And – last but not least – a sense of humour which never deserted him.[83] All these made the partnership with him quite an experience. With the collaboration of the young technicians Antonio Shugt and José Luis Torelli they set to work in an entirely new surface-to-surface missile system that they jokingly called ITB, which stands for *Instalacion de tiro Berreta* – Spanish slang for second-hand firing installation, due to the precariousness of the system – paraphrasing the official name of the system of a warship called ITS (Standard Firing Installation). The central question was how to fool the missile, so that – instead of using the warship's computer that has to send data to the Exocet – a fixed signal would be used as if it were on a ship.

Working against the clock and in total secrecy they created homemade computers that simulated the missile's self-director in order to verify what signals – and how – they reached the missile. The simulator was a copy of the missile container. These tests were carried out on one of the Second World War Argentine destroyers (ARA *Segui*) replacing the entire on-board installation with three boxes (computers) and a series of electronic circuits that were designed and assembled on the spot. The goal was, in short, for the missile to believe that it received the information produced by a complete firing facility of a warship – and not of precarious and manual elements. In just days' work they managed to simulate the entire launch process and verify that the missile received the desired information. Once this was done, they began looking for a generator that could deliver the three-phase voltage required by the system. At that moment they were certain that the ITB could launch, but – to make sure – they made about 15 simulated launches, which theoretically worked correctly.

Simultaneously, in the workshops in Puerto Belgrano – under the direction of Commander Benjamín Dávila, a ramp was built over an old trailer to mount two spare Exocet MM38 missiles with their containers. A second trailer carried a generator – an old 1939 Siemens Searchlight generator, used by the Marine Corps – plus the boxes that formed the ITB. Thus, the state-of-the-art missile launcher was borne. Each trailer weighed around five tons. Commander Pérez volunteered to operate the brand new ITB: he wanted to see if his brand new creature really worked outside the laboratory.

After three attempts, two C-130s of the Argentine Air Force carrying the missile battery landed in Falklands/Malvinas. The land-based Exocet battery was quickly hidden in a shed in Port Stanley, to prevent the islanders reporting its existence to the British. For this reason, they chose to work exclusively at night.

Another difficulty that had to be overcome was a system capable of acquiring a target and providing the correct data to the Exocet. There was no suitable radar for this purpose, so this had to be improvised as well, with an Army RASIT anti-personnel radar operated by Sergeant Eduardo Sanchez of the Argentine Army – the only portable radar available to provide the range to the target, although it was a ground surveillance radar. They soon found out that the systems were incompatible. The RASIT collected target data in metres and miles, requiring a complex conversion to the Exocet´s computer which could only handle degrees of azimuth and a range in kilometres. By using a manual conversion table and a pocket calculator, Pérez succeeded in entering the RASIT data into the Exocet command computer.

The weight of the trailers only allowed them to move along the only paved road between Port Stanley and the airport. To place it in conditions to operate they had to cross the trailer on the road, since it was impossible to do it on the terrain – as it would have sunk irremissibly. The assembly manoeuvre began at dusk, being ready to launch at about 21:00. The disassembly manoeuvre began around 04:00 in order to store the system in a warehouse so that it would not be observed at first light. Thanks to this shim, the British never heard of the existence of the ITB.

Next day, Rear Admiral Otero assigned Lieutenant Edgardo Rodriguez and Lieutenant Mario Abadal to give a hand in the use of the battery. The team was completed with a young Argentine television producer, Carlos Ries Centeno – a former Marine Lieutenant – who was caught accidentally in the islands with a crew, filming documentaries for Channel 13. Pérez explained to everyone how the ITB worked.

On 6 June at 01:00 the RASIT radar locked on a target. They fed the data to the ITB and carried out the launch procedure but the missile did not fire. Pérez suffered a great disappointment but decided to repeat the procedure with the second missile. This time it worked; they had managed to make the first MM38 missile launch from land. The boost of the missile threw Pérez and the two lieutenants several metres back, but for reasons that could not be determined, the missile had not hit the target, making a tight turn to the right. A quick check revealed that due to the precariousness the ITB, to carry out a new launch they had to wait about 20 minutes, in which the condensers of the circuits would be discharged and thus be able to feed new data to the system. In his enthusiasm to hit the target he fired after just 8 minutes.

Next day they requested two more missiles from Puerto Belgrano, which arrived a few days later.

Pérez reviewed the entire system and noted that the 400-cycle power supply did not arrive as it should. With the help of a civilian, he discovered that a voltage regulator diode had burned – ironically, the only English component of the system! Without that little diode, the entire system was useless. Where could they get a replacement in the middle of the Falkland/Malvinas Islands? Pérez, prisoner of great frustration, appeared at the Marine Corps Anti-aircraft Battalion (Lieutenant Commander Hector Silva) where – to his surprise – they had a diode exactly the same as the one he needed. 'It was a miracle!' acknowledged Pérez after the conflict.

They changed the diode and the ITB was operational again. The days passed but now it was the British ships that did not turn up. They had not detected the system but for some strange reason they followed routes that did not pass through the area where the Argentines could get at them with the new coastal battery.

On 12 June at 02:00 a ship entered the ITB firing zone. The efforts of Pérez and his team were about to be rewarded. Pérez tells what happened next: 'In a hurry we carried out the procedure and launched the missile watching it move away in the dark by the glow of the nozzle. Then we saw a short flash … and then an explosion that illuminated the entire horizon and was reflected in the low clouds. The missile had made an impact on [the stern] of the County-class destroyer [HMS *Glamorgan*].'[84] The attack had left a balance of 13 dead and several injured.

The ship had fallen out of action stations a few minutes prior to the missile hit; this caught her unprepared. The missile detonated in the Wessex helicopter hangar, killing eight of the crew instantly. Fuel then flooded through the gaping hole in the deck into the galley, where a steward and four cooks died of burns. However, *Glamorgan* was able to limp away from the scene under her own power but would not take any further part in the campaign.[85]

Two days later – on 14 June – followed the final surrender of all Argentine forces on the islands. Commander Pérez and Lieutenant Rodriguez were about to destroy the ITB with hand grenades, when Rear Admiral Otero stopped them saying: 'Don´t destroy the ITB; the British won´t learn anything new about the Exocet, but they will see that we hit one of their warships with this extraordinary invention of ours, and thus be aware of the skill of the Argentine Navy.'[86]

War reveals a great deal about military institutions, especially the dominant beliefs of each particular service. The South Atlantic conflict revealed that the modest Argentine Navy was able to adapt quickly to modern missile age warfare, while at the same time retained very old notions about naval warfare, which remain valid even in modern combat – although with many caveats. Here are some of these notions:

First, when the Argentine Naval Aviation sank HMS *Sheffield* – one of the most modern destroyers of the Royal Navy – with a single Exocet missile, it inaugurated a new tactic in the annals of naval warfare: the use of air-to-surface missiles by surprise attacks on surface units, a method that attracted the attention of all the navies of the world and generated an unprecedented impact on naval warfare as known until then.

Second, even the old A-4Q Skyhawks piloted with great professionalism and determination managed to repeatedly penetrate the British fleet's anti-aircraft defence systems, thereby demonstrating that even ancient weapons systems can provide significant combat capability when properly used.

Third, the British Task Force never managed to dominate the airspace over the Falkland/Malvinas Islands; otherwise, how can so many losses and the unrestricted use of Port Stanley´s runway until the last day of the conflict be explained? The answer is that their small aircraft carriers had an anti-submarine configuration (ASW) within the framework of the mission assigned by NATO and therefore were not suitable for other important missions such as air defence. The Falklands/Malvinas War showed that the United Kingdom lacked adequate fixed wing aviation and suffered from lack of both airborne early warning and long-range fighters. They barely had 28 Sea Harrier interceptors.

Fourth, many naval analysts believe that the Argentine Navy should have further exploited the advantage of having an aircraft carrier such as the *25 de Mayo*; however they fail to point out that the British also did not expose their ASW aircraft carriers *Hermes* and *Invincible* to a decisive battle because – if they lost any of them – Operation Corporate would have reached an abrupt end. Additionally, the Argentine Navy was very aware of the need to maintain a naval reserve capacity as a defence against a possible post-war Chilean aggression – a possibility that could not be ruled out in 1982.

Finally, and notwithstanding the above, the British naval high command itself admits that until the last day of the war they suspected that the Argentine fleet could attempt a final decisive surface action, which was not possible due to the breakdowns present in most parts of the fleet.[87]

4 CONCLUSION

The author at the ceremony of change of Director of the Argentine Naval Academy in Rio Santiago in May 2013. First on the left in captain's uniform former Lt Juan José Iglesias, the youngest officer of the *Santa Fe* during the war. On the far right, Commander (retired) Horacio Bicain, former CO of the *Santa Fe* during the war. (Author's private collection)

Until August 1990 – when the Persian Gulf War put it into the background – the Falklands/Malvinas War had attracted enormous interest. First came the newspaper accounts, then the first memoirs – most of them written by British senior officers of the Task Force or the land forces who had participated in the campaign – but none translated from Argentina. In the military and naval world painstaking analyses were made, sometimes for the interested public and sometimes for restricted circulation. It was felt at the time that this little war – with its combination of advanced technology and human involvement – was a precursor of things to come. By 1985 the military and naval staffs of all the great powers were well advanced in the publication of histories of the conflict that were intended for the education of their officers. Of these, the British Official History (2005) is probably the best but – as all the others – lacks important Argentine sources. However, apart from its justifiable neglect of the non-military aspects of the war, the Official History makes over-confident use of questionable British and Argentine sources.

As with most wars, the first books to be written (and translated) were not the best; the more thoughtful and reliable accounts too often came after intense public interest had subsided, and they were not translated. Such is the case of the Argentine Navy´s official history – although advertised as unofficial – a volume of 525 pages written by Rear Admiral Argentine Navy (retd) Horacio A. Mayorga and Captain AN (retd) Jorge A. Errecaborde, under the title: *NO VENCIDOS: Relato de las Operaciones Navales en el Conflicto del Atlántico Sur*, edited by Planeta in June 1998. This work was based on a previous classified version from 1986 by the same authors, made by the Combat Actions Analysis Commission (Comisión de Análisis de Acciones de Combate) formed by order of Admiral Anaya after the conflict, with restricted circulation within the Argentine Navy only. This work is based on primary sources never published before and, in general, is quite honest in its conclusions. Even though some facts have been withheld, in some cases – like the chapter on the faulty performance of the torpedoes – it does not hide the Navy´s ultimate responsibility for the setbacks and lack of preparation of this modern weapon system. Another important source is the analysis made by the former Argentine Ambassador in the United Kingdom Vicente E. Berasategui (now retired) in his book *Malvinas: Diplomacia y Conflicto Armado. Comentarios a la historia oficial Britanica*, a single volume of 557 pages edited by Proa Amerian in 2011 which is probably the best case study in Argentina about the diplomatic and military campaign from the Argentine standpoint. The author makes a detailed analysis – chapter by chapter – of Freedman´s official history, pointing out all questionable arguments used by the British with irrefutable evidence.

In this volume a few examples have been noted of distortions that have long been treated as historical evidence, but the main purpose was to draw upon the enormous stock of neglected – mainly Argentine – material. The result is a book which omits – as unreliable – much anecdotal and hitherto unchallenged material recycled in previous works, and which – at the same time – seeks to view the events of 1982 from a new angle: institutional culture.

The Falklands/Malvinas Conflict: A Mission Impossible

There is no doubt at all that for Argentina, the South Atlantic conflict was a traumatic experience. Above all things, the United Kingdom – not Chile – was the wrong enemy, at the wrong time – 1982 – and in the wrong place – the Falkland/Malvinas Islands and South Georgia. As such, it was contrary to many years of defence planning, which had a clear orientation towards an imminent conflict with Chile over the Beagle Channel islands.

The moment freely chosen by the Junta to recover the Falkland/Malvinas Islands primarily benefited the enemy since, in the first place, that bold move implied braking relations with Argentina´s main weapons supplier – the United Kingdom – which had provided the Navy with its most modern naval platforms and new weapons systems. Furthermore, many of the new Argentine warships (MEKO 360 Type destroyers) under construction in West Germany had many British made parts that would be off limits after 2 April 1982.

Choosing your main weapons supplier as an enemy – especially in the case of the Navy – is already something odd, but to engage in a conventional war without waiting the final delivery of the 14 Super Etendard aircraft and the remaining Exocet missiles ordered in France by the government – which were just days away from being delivered to Argentina, as they were to be completed by the end of April 1982 – seems somewhat flawed in the most elementary of common sense. This of course confirms that the Junta operated on its own and did not expect any kind of reaction by the British armed forces after the landing on the Falklands/Malvinas. In addition, the lack of a local defence industry conditioned the development and duration of operations from the very first day.

In terms of weather conditions, it was not the best time of the year (late autumn), a season that made air strike operations extremely difficult – few daylight hours, low clouds, fogs, rain squalls and so forth – especially considering that the air threat was the only weapon system with which Argentina could make a difference vis-a-vis the enemy arsenal.

However, this very nature makes the Falklands/Malvinas conflict so important in a cultural sense because the actions taken by the Argentine Navy were not pre-planned to any significant degree – not even the defence of the islands had been foreseen – and therefore uninhibited by any kind of planning. In this respect, it was an unfettered campaign and many aspects of it reflected improvised or on-the-job solutions.

Table 4: Argentine Servicemen deployed to the Falklands/Malvinas, 1982[1]	
Army	10,001
Navy	3,119
Air Force	1,000
Gendarmeria Nacional	40
Coast Guard	29

Cultural Predilections: Relearning Old Lessons

Wars are in the habit of occurring at a different time and place than expected, contrary to formally foreseen plans or scenarios. The fight must be faced with the forces and equipment available at that time. The Falklands/Malvinas conflict was exactly the type of war that Argentina never thought it would ever have to fight.

The South Atlantic conflict offered a completely different combat scenario from that war-gamed by the Argentine Navy. The primary threat to the Navy was represented by the British hunter-killer nuclear attack submarines and by the Sea Harriers on board the aircraft carriers HMS *Hermes* and HMS *Invincible*. The first made their presence felt in the theatre of operations with the sinking of the old cruiser ARA *General Belgrano* on 2 May 1982. The latter caused the destruction of three Navy A-4Qs and many Argentine Air Force aircraft with the assistance and coordination of the surface ships.

The Argentine Navy, with the sinking of two modern destroyers – HMS *Sheffield* and HMS *Ardent* – and the auxiliary ship – SS *Atlantic Conveyor* – confirmed a very old lesson: that naval air power still remains a major threat to any surface ship in a modern combat environment – in spite of the fact that, in this case, they operated from land bases. With just four Super Etendard fighter bombers and eight Skyhawk A-4Q aircraft, the Navy achieved far superior results to those of the Argentine Air Force, which despite having a much higher number of combat aircraft – 101 – barely achieved a sinking – HMS *Coventry*. The frigate HMS *Antelope* was hit by two bombs – that did not explode – by Skyhawks of Group 5, and by the 3rd Naval Air Squadron in San Carlos Water. During the bomb defusing operations one of them did explode, and the ship caught fire and sank. The Royal Fleet Auxiliary ships – RFA *Sir Galahad* and RFA *Sir Tristram* – were severely damaged by Skyhawks off Fitzroy, but neither of them sank as a result of the strike. Nevertheless, the Argentine Air Force lost 55 brave men during the conflict.

It remains to be seen if this lesson was assimilated by the Navy after 1982, due to the subcultural predilections of the service. This debate goes to the very heart of the Argentine Navy´s institutional culture, because warships have traditionally been the quintessential technology for victory at sea. All of the major cultural icons of the service were experts on surface warfare; however modern naval warfare demonstrated that while the warship or capital ship remains an important platform, the best way to fight – and inflict greater damage to the enemy – came from young naval aviation pilots, either individually or flying in pairs. Furthermore, it highlighted the role of one of the most recent subcultures of the service: The Fleet Air Arm.

For the enemy, the greatest threat was represented in the first place by Argentine Naval Aviation and its fearsome Exocet AM39 surface air missiles and the Super Etendards that carried them, which operated from their bases on the continent. Second were the Argentine submarines, two of which were of the German 209-class – ARA *Salta* and ARA *San Luis* – that were silent and thus very difficult to detect. The Royal Navy, under the influence of possible NATO scenarios, had become a deep-sea anti-submarine force. It had focused on the detection of nuclear submarines by passive acoustic systems. In the South Atlantic, the threat came from small, low-signature, conventional boats. These were unfamiliar conditions for the British, who had to operate anti-submarine warfare teams that relied on passive sonar, not always reliable. So why were there no torpedo hits in the conflict?

After the landing on the Falkland/Malvinas Islands, the Commander of the Submarine Force (Captain Moya Latrubesse) was summoned by Vice Admiral Lombardo to Puerto Belgrano, where he would remain until the end of the war. It is rather odd that none of the more experienced skippers who had served the previous year – most of whom had been posted to Germany – were not summoned to Argentina as quickly as possible, given the urgent need to get the boats operational as soon as possible, especially considering that the Navy only had three boats in active service. Inexplicably the Navy designated the new skippers following normal peacetime procedure. In one case, Captain Moya Latrubesse summoned an officer serving in an administrative post, as was the case of Commander Roberto Salinas who was at the time aide-de-camp to President Galtieri. This officer was ordered to take charge in very short order of the *Salta*, whose skipper had been disembarked on 3 April 1982 due to medical problems. Even more unusual is the fact that the submariners were not ordered to carry out torpedo trials with real combat warheads immediately before or just after the outbreak of war, instead of continuing with the economy of ordinance typical of peacetime. These trials would have alerted the Navy of the serious technical deficiencies that the SST-4 torpedoes had at the time, which jeopardised submarine operations in the South Atlantic. The well justified dismay over this poor performance has obscured a salient fact related to the use of these underwater missiles in submarines. The early days of May 1982 saw many failed torpedo shots, and a controversy erupted over what had caused them. The argument was finally sorted out late that same year: the torpedoes had been carelessly designed and built, and insufficiently tested. Commander Fernando Azcueta in the *San Luis* was aiming them well, but no amount of good aim could get a hit with torpedoes that did not run as touted. By the time the faults were corrected the war was over. The truth is that the Navy had given submarines a very low priority, as evidenced by their small number. Another clear indication that submarines were a secondary element in the cultural preferences of the Navy arises from the analysis of all the tactical exercises carried out between 1974-1981, from which it appears that they primarily served as targets for the surface fleet or were assigned short periods of time for their specific operational training.

In the final analysis, it is clear that the Navy had been given a *mission impossible* for which it was totally unprepared. The warships, captains, and crews were tasked beyond their technological capabilities and the fault lies primarily in a cultural fracture within the service, that allowed its Commander-in-Chief to gamble with the service against a far more powerful and better trained enemy, even though the institution had no combat experience to draw on.

Post war Argentine Defence Policy

The controversy over the Falkland/Malvinas Islands with the United Kingdom has not only been unsolved, but also the British interest in exploiting the oil in the area has increased Argentina's concern. The conventional forces of neighbouring countries are experiencing significant growth in the face of Argentina´s lack of a proper defence policy: the conventional imbalance, therefore, tends to increase.

The recent National Defence Policy Directive made by the Macri administration (2015-2019) maintains a defensive style of warfare approach for the Argentine Republic and has ordered the planning of national defence based on an international scenario that considers that the United States 'has an indisputable military supremacy', and that in the most immediate South American region there is little possibility of interstate conflicts with military consequences. The directive aims to develop an integrated set of military capabilities to ensure national defence, based on a model of *defensive* nature, which authorises to 'eliminate and repel all external military aggression through the use of the Armed Forces'.[2] However, to limit the use of military power to a hypothetical external military aggression from another state, is to adopt a differential criterion between defence and internal security that practically does not exist in any country in the world, where the prevailing concept today is that of asymmetric warfare. For this reason, the current system which is governed by a National Defence Law (N°23,554) and an Internal Security Law (N°24,059) is anachronistic and inadequate to face the threats that the Argentine Republic will have to meet in the next 50 years.

In this regard, former congressman and three times Defence Minister Horacio Jaunarena concluded in a recent work:

> The capacity for aggression by non-state agents … allows us to conclude that the means to be used to respond to an attack do not have to be in relation to the geographical origin of the aggression but rather with the (dangerous) potentiality deployment, among other things. The most modern legislations are quite different from ours regarding the use of the Armed Forces and, consequently, it will be difficult for us to strengthen ties (with third parties) if we remain subordinate to visions that are outdated. That´s why it is necessary to seek a consensus between the different political parties to add to the government agenda the modernization of our defence legislation.[3]

Notwithstanding the foregoing, the execution of the aforementioned directive will also require the intervention of Congress to equip itself with the necessary budget for its implementation, which will give an opportunity to develop a consensus among the major parties on a long-term defence policy. To date that consensus has not been reached and defence policies are conspicuous by their absence.

Unfortunately, a historical analysis of the period 1816-2015 reveals that the moments in which the government reached a political consensus for any given matter have been very rare. The practice and culture in constructing long-term political agreements (or state policies) have been practically non-existent in Argentine history. Strategic planning and the elaboration of certain main lines of action in defence or geopolitical issues in the Southern Cone have been the product of elaborated policies in periods of political hegemony.

However, the internal logic of the political regime prevented the elaboration of an alternative consensual policy.

The Executive has not been endowed with an adequate capacity to articulate long-term policy-making, and the Congress – for the said reasons – has not been able to fulfil this task either. Planning departments at the ministerial level have not existed, nor does the bureaucratic structure or administrative culture of long-term political coordination exist. A paradigmatic case of these problems is the lack of coordinated planning between the Foreign Ministry and the Ministry of Defence: despite the more than 30 years that have elapsed since the democratic restoration, there has been no political will to endow the Ministry of Defence with a body of professionals similar to that of the diplomatic service, nor has there been the will to create between both ministries a common structure of analysis and planning.

However, it should be noted that the successive civilian governments of Argentina have taken political measures aimed at achieving greater coordination and integration between the three armed forces, so that the painful situation that happened in the Falklands/Malvinas conflict does not recur. Among other measures, greater authority and prestige were given to the Joint Chiefs of Staff of the Armed Forces, whose head rotates between the three services – as the heads of departments that depend from it do – Decree N°727/2006 (regulation of Law N°23,554) gave rise to the Operational Command of the Armed Forces to direct and coordinate military activities in peacetime, propose and develop strategic operational planning and conduct operations during crisis situations and in the event of war. The Joint War College (Escuela de Guerra Conjunta) was created in 2007, where the most senior officers of the three services take the Superior Course, which already has several graduates. Additionally, the joint doctrine was rewritten, putting it into practice through successive joint exercises between the armed forces. Finally, some advisory bodies were created to unify defence criteria, such as The Centre for Strategic Defence Studies created by Resolution N°546/2008 of the Ministry of Defence. The task will be arduous and difficult: it takes years to create a new culture, but the country is on the right track.

The current strategic dilemma of Argentina, therefore, is to elucidate on what basis and with what elements should the country be endowed in order to have an adequate deterrent and containment capacity to defend Argentina´s extended sea and land boundaries, maintain a secure regional scenario and actively participate in various multilateral forums where the future of regional power is settled. The current policy of unilateral disarmament is unsustainable and irresponsible, and in no way guarantees that other powers will respect our sovereign rights.

The Future

The start of the 21st century has found the Argentine Navy facing some difficult choices concerning the way ahead, given the political apathy that still persists in successive administrations regarding a much-needed public defence policy. In a well-researched work on defence policy in democratic Argentina, well-known academic and former official of the Defence Ministry, Ruth Diamint concluded that:

> None of the six democratic governments invested in the training of state officials to conduct or administrate defence issues. Society and the media did not assume an active and critical role on the subject. The Congress, more than fulfilling its role as creator of public policy, is caught up in internal disputes. After so many years, defence is still not perceived as a State policy ... A minimal republican architecture ... should lead each institution to fulfil its purpose, grant political stability to the system, and strengthen the political regime. In this context, the exercise of a public defence policy ... is a guarantee for democracy ... and a pillar for a full regional integration.[4]

As former US Secretary of State for Defence Casper Weinberger puts it:

> In the globalized world we live in clearly no nation is strong enough alone to keep its own freedom. Every nation requires alliances, friendships or associations of one kind or another with other countries who share its goals and ideals ... It is not essential that we change our personality as a nation. But we must understand how critically important it is, if we want to keep our democracy, our peace and our freedom, that we be willing to make sacrifices – sacrifices often difficult, expensive, and unpopular. Wise and resolute investment in our military strength is not only consistent with all the blessings of democracy; it is the only course that will let us keep our democracy, our peace and our freedom. If we want peace, we must be willing and able to fight for it.[5]

This is a lesson that Argentina has not yet learned.

There is no doubt that the present economic crisis and the high unemployment rate that is currently plaguing the country have diverted public attention to other issues, focusing on other lower-ranking public policies, such as the immigration of Syrian citizens. That is why it is essential that our legislators commit to the issue, visit our military installations and have an open, fluid and transparent dialogue with the armed forces; otherwise, the path towards a defence policy will never become a state policy.

Navy personnel of all ranks decreased from 32,900 men in 1978 to 18,555 men in 2015.[6] This change is the result of the post-Falklands/Malvinas factor, the end of compulsory military service and the very low budget available to the armed forces today, added to the clear distrust of the political leaders in the military. This fact has given rise to a deep debate on the Navy and its relationship with society.

Another important issue is the critical reduction of surface ships in the fleet, such as the decommission of the aircraft carrier ARA *25 de Mayo* in early 1999; this requires an urgent revision of our defence policy so as to ensure that the Navy complies with her non-delegable mandate, that has been imposed by the nation's constitution. This factor combined with the desertion of personnel due to the low salaries paid by the Navy, and the more attractive jobs offered by the civilian market, makes the Navy lose its traditional appeal for the youngest generations.

Since the end of the Cold War, Argentina has participated in other conflicts, such as the First Gulf War (1990–1991) – this time as an ally of the United Kingdom – and in numerous peace missions sponsored by the United Nations.

The units that integrated the Argentine Task Force that operated in the Persian Gulf between 25 September 1990 and 29 May 1991 during the Menem administration (1989-1999) showed that they could operate at the same level as the rest of the Multinational Force, the material responded above the Navy´s expectations and the implemented logistics system worked fine for such a distant theatre of operations. On this basis, the commander of the Task Force, Captain (later Rear Admiral) Eduardo Rosenthal in his official report concluded:

> The Nation has once again used its naval power in a scenario outside the hemisphere. As in Spanish waters during the civil war and the Caribbean on the occasion of the Cuban missile crisis, the particularity of the use of warships as instruments of State policy has been demonstrated. This meant a prolonged stay in the region of the greatest political crisis today, measuring the commitment made, from combined non-belligerent operations, to the use of surface forces in tasks of close support and protection of combat units.
>
> Having complied with it, strictly maintaining the national command lines, without previous bilateral agreements on permanence and the use of ports on foreign soil and without creating significant interference to the civilian population, can only be achieved with surface forces. The capacity to employ surface forces in an international scenario continues to be a highly relevant tool for the Argentine Republic ...
>
> In another aspect, this conflict revealed that ... the principles of war that they manifested in it continue to be immutable. The use of modern technology in weapons, command and control, and intelligence systems did not cause major surprise or advantage. Here, as in the beginning of the struggle between men, the objective, the initiative, the ability to manoeuvre and the advantage of surprise continue to show that modern warfare technology and the art of war still go hand in hand.[7]

Recent conflicts such as the Afghanistan War and the war on terrorism – of which Argentina has been a target twice – suggests that future wars will be outside the regional sphere in which the Navy normally operates. For this reason, the projection of naval power provided by carrier aviation will be essential in this type of scenario. Therefore, it is necessary for the Navy to acquire an aircraft carrier of 30,000-40,000 tons which could be built in Argentina´s own shipyards. This type of capital ship offers many benefits for the Navy, whether in the short, medium or long term.

First, these platforms are essential for the cultural construction of the force. The capital ship – either consciously or unconsciously – forms the basis on which the Navy relies when it imagines naval warfare – past, present and future. The technology offered by aircraft carriers will allow the Navy to build its belief system in the same way that Brown used his ships to achieve decisive victories. The importance of the capital ship will be ratified and officers can be assured that the technology that has provided the service with its greatest successes through the centuries will once again be at their disposal. One of the complementary benefits of owning these large ships will be their impact on Argentine society as a whole: the aircraft carriers and their multi-aircraft wing are very attractive. Newspapers and other media outlets have given relevance – in various crises – to the movements of aircraft carriers. It is the giant of the sea; the air base that moves from one place to another, capable of deterring with its timely presence in the right place at the right time. Reinforcing that tangible presence are the surface ships that accompany it, complementing its defensive and offensive capabilities. The aircraft carrier is the pinnacle of operational flexibility, all the more so as its size allows it to have a large air group consisting of various types of aircraft. The weapons and eyes of the aircraft carrier are its aircraft; that is why it is often said that its guns are by far the longest range and its means of detection are those that scan the furthest. The aircraft carrier is today the essence of naval power. Its possession or absence is one of the factors that mark the rank of a fleet.

An Institutional Culture for the 21st Century

Surprisingly, despite the profound changes in the size and force structure of the Argentine Navy and the doctrinal changes introduced since the end of the Cold War, the institutional culture of the service has hardly altered. The beliefs that have served the Argentine Navy so well in the past continue to be replicated at the initial training establishment, the often little-recognised *Escuela Naval Militar*. The memory of cultural icons and long-standing traditions within the institution are very much alive within the officer corps. In many ways, these cultural trends are a healthy sign that – despite the immense technological and societal changes that have occurred in the last 40 years – the institution has not lost sight of its original purpose: to train leaders for the defence of the homeland at sea, and above all things, contribute – with the other armed forces – to obtain victory at sea for the Argentine state. The future of modern warfare in light of the terrorist threat is uncertain, and the Navy is currently facing major changes in its internal structure, but there is no doubt that naval officers will adapt to the challenges ahead in the same manner as their forebears.

Thirty-eight years after the South Atlantic conflict, it can be concluded that the Argentine Navy successfully passed her very much-delayed combat test. Despite notable difficulties and internal tensions, the Navy did quite a lot of damage with very little. The Argentine Navy played a fundamental role in the fight and accounted for a significant part of the enemy forces. However, this valuable and traumatic experience has been wasted by the government, which has shown itself incapable of conceiving a defence policy to safeguard its national interests and contribute to maintain a regional balance of power. The basic conclusion that can be drawn from this research is that the Falklands/Malvinas Conflict meant a cultural fracture for the Argentine Navy that will never ever happen again. Additionally, it can be affirmed that the Navy will continue to reflect – in peacetime as well as in wartime – its cultural predilections. It remains to be seen in future campaigns if it is a winning formula.

BIBLIOGRAPHY

Interviews and Correspondence

Admiral (retd) Jorge Isaac Anaya
Admiral (retd) Daniel Alberto E. Martin
Admiral (retd) Emilio Molina Pico
Vice Admiral (retd) Carlos Luis Alfonso
Vice Admiral (retd) Juan José Lombardo
Vice Admiral (retd) Benito Rótolo
Rear Admiral (retd) Ricardo Luis Alessandrini
Rear Admiral (retd) Carlos A. Büsser
Rear Admiral (retd) Oscar C. Fernández Osuna
Rear Admiral (retd) Julio Marcelo Pérez
Rear Admiral (retd) Carlos Maria Sala
Rear Admiral (retd) Carlos Alfredo Vaihinger
Captain (retd) Ricardo Aumann
Captain (retd) Fernando Maria Azcueta
Captain (retd) Washington Barcena
Captain (retd) Horacio Conrad
Captain (retd) Alfredo Raúl Cufré Ricardo
Captain (retd) Benjamín Dávila
Captain (retd) Horacio Grassi César
Captain (retd) Julio Eneas Grosso
Captain (retd) Juan José Iglesias
Captain (retd) Jorge Horacio Papa
Captain (retd) José Alberto Somonte
Captain (retd) Alejandro J. Tierno
Captain (retd) César Trombetta
Commander (retd) Horacio Alberto Bicain
Commander (retd) Horacio Justo Gómez Beret
Commander (retd) Luis Carlos Lagos
Lieutenant Commander (retd) Benjamín Argañaras
Lieutenant Commander (retd) Juan Carlos Segura
First Lieutnenant (retd) Guillermo J. Luna
First Lieutnenant I.M. (retd) Gustavo Richardson
Chief Petty Officer (retd) Héctor Felman
Petty Officer (retd) Leonardo Dante Francescone
Commodore, Argentine Air Force (retd) Eduardo Gómez
Lieutenant Coronel, Royal Marine (retd) Guy Sheridan
Major (retd), Royal Marine, Ewen Southby-Tailyour
Lieutenant Commander (retd), Royal Navy, Tony Ellerbeck
Lieutenant Commander (retd), Royal Navy, Bill Hurst
Lieutenant Commander (retd), Royal Navy, Andrew Lockett
Assistant Marine Supt., Royal Maritime Auxiliary Service, Jason Small

Unpublished Documents

Vice Adm Lombardo, Juan José (retd), *Malvinas: Errores, anécdotas y reflexiones* (unpublished manuscript)
Reconquista de las Islas Georgias del Sur -1982- Publicación Interna del Comando de la Infantería Marina
Islas Georgias del Sur, fase defensa y caída -1982- Oficina Malvinas del Comando de la Infantería de Marina
Proceso N°1/982 "S" JIES, SFE que tramitara ante el Juzgado de Instrucción Militar Especial N°1 (CSFA) instruido con motivo de: Submarino Santa Fe: determinación de las circunstancias en que se produjeron las averías, el abandono, la captura, el hundimiento del buque y deslindar la responsabilidad del Comandante de la Unidad.
Vice Adm Lombardo, Juan José (retd), *Informe oficial elevado al JEMGA* (Archivo General de la Armada)
Vice Adm Lombardo, Juan José, *Informe sobre las acciones cumplidas por el submarino ARA Santa Fe en las Islas Georgias del Sur elevado por el Vicealmirante Juan José Lombardo, Comandante de Operaciones Navales, al Señor Jefe del Estado Mayor General de la Armada con fecha 13 de Julio de 1982.*

Articles

Vice Adm Alfonso, Carlos (retd), 'La Corbeta ARA Guerrico y el conflicto Austral', *Boletín del Centro* Naval, N°832 (Jan-Apr 2012), pp.49-63
Adm Anaya, Jorge (retd), 'Letter to Admiral Sandy Woodward on 07 May 1991', in *Boletín del Instituto de Numismática y Antigüedades*, separata N°19 *Malvinas: mitos y realidades*, (1998), pp.64-65
Adm Anaya, Jorge (retd), 'Secret memorándum to Admiral Ramón Aroza on 6 June 1984', in *Archivo General de la Armada*, p.13
Adm Anaya, Jorge (retd), 'Speech at Consejo Supremo de las Fuerzas Armadas on 30 March 1983', in *Gente*, N°959 (8 Dec 1983), p.18
Adm Anaya, Jorge (retd), statement from 22 Apr 1983 reproduced in *Gente*, N°959 (8 Dec 1983), p.90
Vice Adm Alfonso, Carlos (retd), 'La corbeta Guerrico y el conflicto Austral', *Boletín del Centro Naval*, N°832 (Jan-Apr 2021), pp.49-52
Bóveda, Jorge R., 'El Secreto del ARA Salta', *Todo es Historia*, N° 417 (Apr 2002), pp.28-31
Bóveda, Jorge R., 'ARA Salta´s Secret', *Warship World*, vol. 7 N°10 (Mar 2002), p.13-15
Bóveda, Jorge R., 'Helicópteros del Ejército en Acción', *Todo es* Historia, N°489 (Apr 2008), p.66-76
Bóveda, Jorge R., 'Operación Plum Duff', *Boletín del Centro Naval*, N°840 (Jan–June 2015), p.82
Bóveda, Jorge R., 'Rescatando al Clipper Adventurer: una operación sin precedentes del Rompehielos Alte. Irizar', *Boletín del Centro* Naval, N°835 (2013), pp.49-58
Bóveda, Jorge R., 'Submarinos en Malvinas', *Fuerza Naval [España]*, vol. III N°26 and N°27 (2004)
Bóveda, Jorge R., 'Un Marino de Fin de Siglo: Contraalmirante Manuel José García-Mansilla, su vida, su obra y su tiempo', *Suplemento del Boletín del Centro Naval*, N°827 (2010)
Bóveda, Jorge R., 'Uno contra todos', *Boletín del Centro* Naval, N°816 (Jan-Apr 2007), pp.113-126
Rear Adm Büsser, Carlos, Interview: Çómo se planificó la acción, *Revista Noticias - Malvinas Diez años después*, (26 Mar 1991), p.70
Cable, Sir James, 'The Falklands Conflict', *Proceedings*, (Sept 1982), pp.71-76
Cable, Sir James, 'Who was surprised in the Falklands and why?', *Encounter*, (Sep–Oct 1982), pp.30-42
Campbell, Duncan, 'Falklands War: The Chilean connection', *New Stateman*, (25 Jan 1985)
Castrillón, Emilio and Casabal, Luis, 'Nostalgias de Olor a Nafta Quemada', *La Nación*, (7 Sept 1997), p.3

Castrillón, Emilio and Casabal, Luis, 'Fuego sobre el Atlántico Sur', *La Nación, sección Enfoques*, (7 Sept 1997), p.2

Castro Fox, Rodolfo, 'La Tercera Escuadrilla Aeronaval de Caza y Ataque a 25 años del Conflicto del Atlántico Sur', *Boletín del Centro Naval*, N°817 (May–Aug 2007), pp.227-234

Capt Cohen, José M., 'Necesidad del Poder Naval, estrategia naval y medios', *Revista de la Escuela de Guerra Naval*, N°10 (Feb 1979), p.123

Capt Cohen, José M., 'Tres Temas de estrategia Naval', *Boletín del Centro Naval*, N°692 (July–Sept 1972), pp.297-298

Capt Coli, Carlos A. (retd), 'La Flota de Mar en la Guerra del Atlántico Sur: su actuación posterior al 2 de abril de 1982', *Boletín del Centro Naval*, N°818 (Sept–Dic 2007), pp.87-108

Delamer, Guillermo, Montenegro, Guillermo, Bergallo, Jorge y Santillán, Haroldo, 'Evolución del Pensamiento Estratégico Naval Argentino a lo largo de la Historia' Parte 1, *Boletín del Centro Naval*, N°828 (Sept–Dic 2010), p.215

del Carril, Bonifacio, 'Cómo se perdió la paz en 1982', *La Nación, sección Enfoques*, (4 Apr 1999), p.1-2

Diamint, Rut, 'Entrevista', *La Nación*, (22 Mar 2015), p.4

Dojas, Albert E. 'Una reflexión sobre nuestra cultura estratégica', *Revista Temas de Política Exterior, Comercio y Relaciones Exteriores, Asociación Profesional del Servicio Exterior de la Nación*, Año IV N°4 (Dec 2011)

Escudé, Carlos, '¿Somos un Protectorado de Chile y Brasil?', *La Nación*, (24 Jan 2013), p.21

Figueroa, Alberto, 'La vida a bordo de un gigante', Revista *La Semana*, (5 Dec 1979), pp.60–67

Capt Figueroa, Álvaro (retd), 'Malvinas: las fallas de la guerra: análisis de caso: combate de Grytviken', *Revista de la Escuela de Guerra Naval*, N°59 (Dec 2013), pp.117-133

Finlan, Alastair, 'British Special Forces and the Falklands Conflict: Twenty years on', *Defence & Security Analysis*, vol. 18 N°4 (2002), pp.319-333

Freedman, Lawrence, 'Intelligence Operations in the Falklands', *Intelligence and National Security*, vol. 1 N°3 (Sept 1986)

Giavedoni Pita, Manuel, 'La Estrategia Hoy. Releyendo a José Maria Cohen', *Boletín del Centro Naval*, N°820 (Apr–June 2008), pp.161-172

Gray, Colin S., 'Strategic Culture as Context: The First Generation of Theory Strikes Back', *Review of International Studies*, (25 Jan 1999), pp.49-69

Hurrell, Andrew, 'The Politics of South Atlantic Security: a Survey of Proposals for a South Atlantic Organization', *International Affairs*, vol. 59 N°2 (Spring 1983), pp.179-193

Jenkins, Simon, 'Interview', *Clarín, suplemento Zona* (8 Apr 2007), pp.32-33

Lazzari, Emilio, 'La Urdimbre vital', *Boletín del Centro Naval*, N°775 (1994), pp.578-582

Legro, Jeffrey W., 'Military Culture and Inadvertent Escalation in World War II', *International Security*, (1984), pp.108-142

Macmillan, Allan, 'Strategic Culture and National Ways in Warfare: The British Case', *RUSI* Journal, Vol.140 N°5 (1995), pp.33-38

Makin, Guillermo, 'The military in Argentine Politics:1880–1982', *Millennium: Journal of International Studies 12*, vol. 6 N°1 (Spring 1983), pp.49-68

Makin, Guillermo, 'Argentine approaches to the Falklands/Malvinas: Was the resort to force foreseeable?', *International Affairs*, vol. 59 N°3 (1983), pp.391-403

Malamud, Marina, 'Sociología Militar', *Boletín del Centro Naval*, N°837 (Sept–Dec 2013), p.384

Milia, Fernando, 'La Armada Argentina: un perfil socio-político', *Boletín del Centro* Naval, N°758–759 (1989), pp.489-498

Moore, Jeremy and Woodward, John, 'The Falklands Experience', *Royal United Services Institute Journal*, (Mar 1983)

Mozzarelli, Antonio J., 'El Grupo Naval en las Islas Malvinas', *Boletín del Centro Naval*, N°783 (1996), p.585

Mozzarelli, Antonio J., 'Nuestra Fuerza de Submarinos: una vieja falencia de nuestro poder naval', *Revista Argentina de Estudios Estratégicos*, N°18 (May1998), pp.33-49

Pérez, Julio 'Operación Uka Uka', *Boletín del Centro Naval*, N°820 (Apr–June 2008), pp.211-217

Rear Adm Robacio, Carlos H.(retd), 'El Batallón de Infantería de Marina 5 en Malvinas', *Boletín del Centro Naval*, Vol. N°735 (1983), p.145

Lt Cdr Robles, Miguel, 'Interview', *La Semana* magazine, (5 Dec 1979), pp.60–67

Graciela Romer, 'Wenceslao Bunge Interview: 'Malvinas: from a diplomatic victory to a military defeat', *Actualización Política*, (April–May 1992), p.74

Rosenthal, Eduardo, 'La Armada Argentina en el Golfo Pérsico', *Boletín del Centro Naval*, N°763 (1991), p.255-267

Russell, David, 'How Exocet sank the HMS *Sheffield*', *Defense Electronics*, (July 1982), pp.43-47

Sciaroni, Mariano, 'Alerta Temprana desde submarinos: la experiencia de la Royal Navy', *Revista de la Escuela de Guerra Naval*, N°58 (Oct 2012), pp.61-73

Sciaroni, Mariano, 'Satélites norteamericanos sobre las islas Malvinas', *Revista de la Escuela de Guerra Naval* N°62 (Dec 2016), pp.119-134

Scheina, Robert L., 'The Malvinas Campaign', *Proceedings: Naval Review*, (Mar 1983), pp.98-117

Scheina, Robert L., 'Where were those Argentine Subs', *Proceedings*, (Mar 1984), pp.115-120

Sicalesi, Juan Carlos and Rivas, Santiago, 'El hundimiento de la HMS *Ardent*', Fuerza Naval,

España, MC Ediciones, año V, vol. 6 N°57, (2002), pp.63-64

Lt Col Svendsen, Jorge (retd), 'Acciones helitransportadas', in Lt Gen Martín Balza (retd) (coord.), Malvinas, Relatos de soldados, *Biblioteca del Suboficial*, vol. 154 (1986), pp.43-44

Capt Sylvester, Ricardo (retd), 'Interview', *in Defensa y Seguridad*, Año 6 N°30 (Mar–Apr 2006), p.20

Train, Harry (Adm USN), 'Malvinas, un caso de estudio', *Boletín del Centro Naval*, N°834 (Sept–Dic 2012), p.238

Trombetta, César, 'Ocupación de las islas Georgias durante el conflicto del Atlántico Sur en 1982', *Boletín del Centro Naval*, N°735 (1983), pp.105-115

Urien, Paula, 'La carrera militar, un camino en busca de definiciones', *La Nación*, (15 Sept 2013), p.11

Wilbur, Charles H., 'Remember the San Luis!', *Proceedings*, (Mar 1996)

Juan Yofre, 'Leopoldo F. Galtieri Interview', *Clarín, Suplemento especial* (2 Apr 1983)

Selected Bibliography

Anon, *Centésimo Aniversario de la Escuela Naval Militar* (Buenos Aires: Publisher unknown, 1972)

Arguindeguy Pablo y Rodríguez Horacio, *Las Fuerzas Navales Argentinas: historia de la flota de mar* (Buenos Aires: Instituto Browniano, 1995)
Autores varios, *Libro Blanco de la Defensa Nacional* (Buenos Aires: Ministerio de Defensa, 2010)
Barker, Nick, *Beyond Endurance: An Epic of Whitehall and the South Atlantic Conflict* (London: Leo Cooper, 1997)
Barnett, Roger W., *Navy Strategic Culture: why the navy thinks differently* (Annapolis, Maryland: USNI Press, 2009)
Bignone, Reynaldo, *El Último de facto: la liquidación del proceso* (Buenos Aires: Editorial Planeta, 1992)
Bonzo, Héctor, *1093 Tripulantes del Crucero ARA General Belgrano* (Buenos Aires: Instituto de Publicaciones Navales, 2004)
Bóveda, Jorge R., *Malvinas: la odisea del Submarino Santa Fe* (Buenos Aires: Instituto de Publicaciones Navales, 2007)
Bransby, Guy, *Her Majesty's Interrogator Falklands* (London: Leo Cooper, 1996)
Brodie, Bernard, *A Layman´s Guide to Naval Strategy* (Oxford: Oxford University Press, 1943)
Brodie, Bernard, *War & Politics* (London: Cassell, 1973)
Brown, David, *The Royal Navy and the Falklands War* (London: Leo Cooper, 1988)
Burden, Rodney A., et al, *Falklands: the Air War* (London: Arms & Armour Press, 1987)
Rear Adm Büsser Carlos (retd), *Operación Rosario*, 2da ed. ampliada y corregida (Buenos Aires: Asociación de Oficiales Retirados de la Infantería de Marina, 1999)
Cable, Sir James, *Britain´s Naval Future* (Annapolis, Maryland: Naval Institute Press, 1983)
Cable, Sir James, *Gunboat Diplomacy 1919-1991: Political Applications of Limited Naval Force* (London: Macmillan, 1971)
Capt Carballo, Pablo, *Dios y los Halcones* (Buenos Aires: Ediciones Rex, 1999)
Cardoso, Oscar, Kirschbaum, Ricardo and Van der Kooy, Eduardo, *Malvinas: La trama Secreta* (Buenos Aires: Sudamericana-Planeta, 1983)
Castro Fox, Rodolfo, *Yo fui piloto aviador naval* (Buenos Aires: Círculo Militar, 2002)
Cavallieri, Daniel, *Hasta la Última Balsa* (Buenos Aires: Instituto de Publicaciones Navales, 2011)
Churchill, Sir Winston L., *The World Crisis: 1911-1918* (abridged and revised ed.) (New York: Free Press, 2005)
Clapp, Michael, *Amphibious Assault Falklands: The Battle for San Carlos Water* (Annapolis, Maryland: Naval Institute Press, 1996)
Cooper, T. & Sipos, M., *Iraqi Mirages: the Dassault Mirage Family in Service with the Iraqi Air Force, 1981-1988* (Warwick: Helion & Co., 2019)
Corbett, Julian S., *Some Principles of Maritime Strategy* (London: LLM Longmans Green and Co., 1911)
Craig, Chris, *Call for Fire: Sea Combat in the Falklands and the Gulf War* (London: John Murray Publishers, 1995)
Diamint, Rut, *Sin Gloria: la Política de Defensa en la Argentina Democrática* (Buenos Aires: Eudeba, 2014)
Dillon, G.M., *The Falklands: Politics and War* (London: Macmillan Press, 1989)
Doratioto, Francisco, *Maldita Guerra. Nueva historia de la Guerra del Paraguay* (Buenos Aires: Emecé, 2004)
Escudé, Carlos, *La Argentina: ¿Paria Internacional?* (Buenos Aires: Editorial de Belgrano, 1984)
Escudé, Carlos, *La Argentina vs. Las Grandes Potencias: el precio del desafío* (Buenos Aires: Editorial de Belgrano, 1986)
Ethell, Jeffrey and Price Alfred, *Air War South Atlantic* (London: Sidgwick & Jackson, 1983)
Fraga, Rosendo, *¿Qué hubiera pasado si…?* (Buenos Aires: Editorial Vergara, 2008)
Figallo, Beatriz, *Diplomáticos y Marinos Argentinos durante la Crisis Española. Los Asilos en la Guerra Civil* (Buenos Aires: Librería Histórica, 2007)
Finlan Alastair, *The Royal Navy in the Falklands Conflict and the Gulf War: Culture & strategy* (London: Frank Cass, 2004)
Freedman, Lawrence and Gamba-Stonehouse, Virginia, *Signals of War: The Falklands Conflict of 1982* (New Jersey: Princeton University Press, 1991)
Gamba, Virginia, *The Falklands/Malvinas War: A model for North-South Crisis Prevention* (London: Allen & Unwin Inc., 1987)
Gilobert, Héctor, in R. Palazzi, *Malvinas: Otras Historias* (Buenos Aires: Editorial Claridad, 2006)
Hart Dyke, David, *Four Weeks in May* (London: Atlantic Books, 2007)
Hatch, Mary Jo, *Organization Theory: Modern, Symbolic, and Postmodern Perspectives* (Oxford: Oxford University Press, 1997)
Hastings, Max and Jenkins, Simon, *The Battle for the Falklands* (London: Book Club Associates, 1983)
Hughes, Wayne, *Fleet Tactics: Theory and Practice* (Annapolis, Maryland: Naval Institute Press, 1986)
Inskip, Ian, *Ordeal by Exocet: HMS Glamorgan and the Falklands War 1982* (London: Greenhill books, 2006)
Jaunarena, Horacio, *La Casa está en orden: memoria de la transición* (Buenos Aires: Editorial Taeda, 2011)
Johnston, Alastair I., *Cultural Realism: Strategic Culture and Grand Strategy in Chinese History* (New Jersey: Princeton University Press, 1995)
Keegan, John, *Intelligence in War: Knowledge of the enemy from Napoleon to Al-Qaeda* (New York: Alfred A. Knopf, 2003)
Kemp, Anthony, *The SAS Savage Wars of Peace, 1947 to the Present* (Kolkata, West Bengal: Signet, 1995)
Kilmann, Ralph, Saxton, Mary J. and Serpa, Roy, *Gaining Control of the Corporate Culture* (San Francisco: Jossey-Bass, 1985)
Macmillan, Alan, 'Culture and Conflict in the Post-Cold War World', in M. Janes Davis (ed.), *Security Issues in the Post-Cold War World* (Cheltenham, UK: Edward Elgar, 1996)
Captain (RN) Bob McQueen, *Ascension Island in the Falklands War* (Scotland: Whittles Publishing, 2007)
Mahan, Alfred T., *The Influence of Sea Power Upon History 1660-1783* (London: Sampson Low, 1892)
Maisonneuve, Charles and Razoux, Pierre, *La Guerre des Malouines* (Clichy, hauts de Seine: Editions Lariviere, 2002)
Martini, Héctor, *Historia de la Aviación Naval Argentina: Conflicto del Atlántico Sur, Tomo III* (Buenos Aires: Departamento de Estudios Históricos Navales, 1992)
Mayorga, Horacio, *No Vencidos: relato de las operaciones navales en el conflicto del Atlántico Sur* (Buenos Aires: Editorial Planeta, 1998)

Brig Maj Menéndez, Mario (retd), *Malvinas: testimonio de su gobernador* (Buenos Aires: Editorial Sudamericana, Buenos Aires, 1983)

Fuchida, Mitsuo and Okumiya Masatake, *Midway* (Buenos Aires: Instituto de Publicaciones Navales, 2002)

Middlebrook, Martin, *The Fight for the Malvinas: The Argentine Forces in the Falklands War* (London: Viking, 1989)

Middlebrook, Martin, *Task Force: The Falklands War, 1982* (London: Penguin Books, 1987)

Muñoz, Jorge, *Misión Cumplida: Historia de la Marina Mercante en el Conflicto del Atlántico Sur* (Buenos Aires: Editorial Epopeya, 2000)

Muñoz, Jorge, *Poker de Ases en Malvinas* (Buenos Aires: Instituto de Publicaciones Navales, 2004)

Paret, Peter (ed.), *Makers of Modern Strategy: from Machiavelli to the Nuclear Age* (Oxford: Clarendon, 1986)

Perkins, Roger, *Operation Paraquat: The Battle for South Georgia* (Chippenham: Picton Publishing, 1986)

Scheina Robert L., *Latin America: A Naval History 1810-1987* (Annapolis, Maryland: Naval Institute Press, 1987)

Schein, Edgar H., *Organizational Culture and Leadership* (Oxford: Jossey-Bass, 1991)

Sciaroni, Mariano, *Malvinas, tras los submarinos ingleses* (Buenos Aires: Instituto de Publicaciones Navales, 2013)

Col Seineldín, Mohamed A., *Malvinas un sentimiento* (Buenos Aires: Editorial Sudamericana, 1999)

Southby-Tailyour, Ewen, *Exocet Falklands: The Untold Story of Special Forces Operations* (London: Pen & Sword Military, 2014)

Storni, Segundo, *Intereses Argentinos en el Mar* (Buenos Aires: Ministerio de Defensa, 2009)

Thompson, Julian, *No Picnic: 3 Commando Brigade in the South Atlantic: 1982* (London: Leo Cooper for Secker & Warburg, 1985)

Thatcher, Margaret, *The Downing Street Years* (London: Harper Collins, 1993)

Till, Geoffrey, *Maritime Strategy and the Nuclear Age* (London: Palgrave Macmillan Press Ltd, 1984)

Till, Geoffrey, *Seapower: A Guide for the Twenty-First Century* (New York: Routledge, 2009)

Von Clausewitz, Carl, in F.N. Maude (ed.), *On War* (London: Kegan Paul, Trench, Trübner and Co., 1911)

Ward, Sharkey, *Sea Harrier over the Falklands* (Annapolis, Maryland: Naval Institute Press, 1992)

Weinberger, Caspar, *Fighting for Peace* (New York: Warner Books, 1990)

West, Nigel, *The Secret War for the Falklands* (London: Little, Brown & Company, 1997)

Winton, John, *Signals from the Falklands* (London: Leo Cooper, 1995)

Woodward, Sandy and Robinson, Patrick, *One Hundred Days* (Annapolis, Maryland: Naval Institute Press, 1997)

Official Reports

Franks, Lord Oliver S., *Falkland Islands review: Report of a Committee of Privy Counsellors.* Cmnd 8787 (London: HMSO, 1983)

Freedman, Lawrence, *The Official History of the Falklands Campaign* vol.I and II (Abingdon: Routledge, 2005)

Rattenbach, Benjamín, *Informe de la Comisión de Análisis y evaluación de las responsabilidades políticas y estratégico militares en el Conflicto del Atlántico Sur* (Buenos Aires: Ediciones Fin de Siglo, 2000)

House of Commons, *Fourth Report of the Defence Committee, Session 1986-87, Implementing the lessons of the Falklands Campaign*, vol. I and II (London: HMSO, 1987)

Great Britain. Ministry of Defence, *The Falklands Campaign: The lessons.* Cmnd 8738 (London: HMSO, 1982)

NOTES

Chapter 1

1 See: Beatriz Figallo, *Diplomáticos y Marinos Argentinos durante la Crisis Española. Los Asilos en la Guerra Civil* (Buenos Aires: Librería Histórica, 2007).
2 That said, and as described in Cooper et al, *Iraqi Mirages* (see bibliography for details), the first to deploy air-launched AM39 Exocets in combat were the Iraqi Air Force and the Iraqi Navy: the former had a unit equipped with French-made Aérospatiale SA.321 Super Frelon Helicopters, which – after being subjected to the control of the Iraqi Navy – were the first to deploy at least a dozen AM39s against ships involved in convoy-operations along the Iranian coast. The first confirmed hit by an air-launched Exocet in combat was scored in October 1981 – more than six months before the Falklands/Malvinas War.
3 Rosenthal, 'La Armada Argentina', pp.255-267.
4 Bóveda, 'Rescatando al Clipper Adventurer, pp.49-58.
5 Anon, *Centésimo Aniversario*, p.9.
6 Bóveda, 'Un Marino de Fin de Siglo', separata.
7 Bóveda, 'Un Marino de Fin de Siglo', separata.
8 Delamer, et al., 'Evolución', p.215.
9 Ministerio de Defensa, *Libro Blanco*, p.9.
10 Storni, *Intereses*, p.3.
11 Escudé, 'Somos', p.21.
12 Diamint, 'Entrevista', p.4.
13 Malamud, 'Sociología', p.384.
14 Urien, 'La carrera', p.11.
15 art. 1 Decree 683/2018.
16 Brodie, *War*, p.377.
17 Kilmann, *Gaining Control*, p.11.
18 Johnston, *Cultural Realism*, p.35.
19 Decree 503/2015 declassified all Argentine documents related to the Falklands/Malvinas War.
20 The author was admitted as an Officer Cadet in the Naval Academy in January 1980 until the end of that year.
21 Legro, 'Military Culture', pp.108-142.
22 Finlan, *The Royal Navy*, p.5.
23 Finlan, *The Royal Navy*, p.7.
24 Finlan, *The Royal Navy*, p.7.
25 Finlan, *The Royal Navy*, p.7.
26 Ministerio de Defensa, *Libro Blanco*, p.108.
27 Doratioto, *Maldita Guerra*, p.130.
28 Milia, 'La Armada Argentina', pp.489-498.
29 Milia, 'La Armada Argentina', p.494.
30 Women were admitted at the Argentine Naval Academy from 2002 onwards, however the scope of this analysis reaches until only 1982.
31 Lazzari, 'La Urdimbre vital', pp.578-582.
32 Hatch, *Organization Theory*, p.214.
33 Argentine Constitution, art. 99 § 12.
34 Cable, 'Who was surprised', pp.30-42.
35 Gilobert, 'Malvinas: Otras Historias', pp.236-238.
36 Adm Jorge Anaya (retd), interview, 1 Nov 2006.
37 Vice Adm Juan Lombardo (retd), *Malvinas*, p.44.
38 Adm Jorge Anaya (retd), interview, 1 Nov 2006.
39 Adm Anaya, 'Speech,' 30 Mar 1983.
40 Vice Adm Lombardo (retd), *Malvinas*, p.44.
41 Fraga, *¿Qué hubiera pasado*, p.329.
42 Fraga, *¿Qué hubiera pasado*, p.329.
43 Vice Adm Lombardo (retd), *Malvinas*, p.40.
44 This belongs to an interview the author made with a high-ranking Argentine diplomat who was part of Costa Méndez's cabinet and close friend of his, who asked to remain anonymous. See also: former President Galtieri, interview, 2 Apr 1983, and Bunge, interview, Apr-May 1992, where it is acknowledged that ambassador Ortiz de Rozas advised that Britain would not react militarily.
45 del Carril, 'Cómo se perdió', p.1.
46 Adm Anaya, 'Secret memorándum', p.13.
47 Trombetta, 'Ocupación', pp.105-115.
48 Rattenbach, *Informe*, p.62.
49 Escudé, *La Argentina*, p.61.
50 Adm Anaya, 'Letter', pp.64-65.
51 The Supreme Council of the Armed Forces, chaired by Lieutenant General Benjamín Rattenbach, tried the Malvinas case and imposed upon Admiral Jorge Anaya, Lieutenant General Leopoldo Galtieri and Brigadier General Basilio Lami Dozo sentences of 14, 12, and eight years of imprisonment respectively, plus the accessory of dismissal. The sentence was appealed to the Federal Court which reduced the penalty set for each one to 12 years of imprisonment, plus the accessory of dismissal for each prosecuted. The defendants filed an Extraordinary Appeal before the Supreme Court. In these circumstances before the Court was issued the Executive (President Menem) in use of its constitutional powers, issued Decree 1005/89 (6 Oct 1989) with a pardon for the three commanders alleging reasons of a higher legal order, tending to contribute to a true reconciliation and national pacification.

Chapter 2

1 Bignone, *El Último*, pp.93-94.
2 Cable, 'The Falklands', pp.71-76.
3 Macmillan, 'Strategic Culture', pp.33-38.
4 Macmillan, 'Strategic Culture', p.34.
5 See: Escudé Carlos, *Gran Bretaña, Estados Unidos y la Declinación Argentina 1942–1949* (Buenos Aires: Editorial de Belgrano, 1983).
6 Escudé, *La Argentina:*, pp.55-63.
7 Escudé, *La Argentina vs. las Grandes*, p.270.
8 André Beaufre in Barnett, *Navy Strategic Culture*, p.65.
9 Arguindeguy et al., *Las Fuerzas*, p.225.
10 Arguindeguy et al., *Las Fuerzas*, p.225.
11 Arguindeguy et al., *Las Fuerzas*, p.225.
12 Arguindeguy et al., *Las Fuerzas*, p.225.
13 Hurrell, 'The Politics', pp.179-193.
14 Hurrell, 'The Politics', pp.179-193.
15 Capt J.M. Cohen in Giavedoni Pita, 'La Estrategia Hoy.', pp.161-172.
16 Capt J.M. Cohen in M. Giavedoni Pita, 'La Estrategia Hoy.', pp.161-172.
17 Scheina, *Latin America*, p.176.
18 Scheina, *Latin America*, pp.175-176.
19 Capt Cohen, 'Letter' in Scheina, *Latin America*, p.176.
20 Scheina, *Latin America*, p.176.
21 Barnett, *Navy Strategic Culture*, p.7.
22 Barnett, *Navy Strategic Culture*, p.7.
23 Barnett, *Navy Strategic Culture*, p.44.

24 Barnett, *Navy Strategic Culture*, p.45.
25 Barnett, *Navy Strategic Culture*, p.45.
26 Capt Cohen, 'Necesidad del Poder Naval', p.123.
27 Finlan, *The Royal Navy*, pp.46-47.
28 Corbett, *Some Principles*, pp.211-214.
29 Russell, 'How Exocet', pp.43-47.
30 Till, *Seapower*, p.169.
31 Cable, *Gunboat Diplomacy*, p.31.
32 *The Telegraph* 7 May 1982 cited in Till, *Maritime Strategy*, p.263.
33 Cable, *Gunboat Diplomacy*, p.8.
34 M. Howard in Till, *Maritime Strategy*, p.266.
35 Capt (RN) McQueen, *Ascension*, pp.11-12.
36 M. Howard in Till, *Maritime Strategy*, p.269.
37 Gamba, *The Falklands/Malvinas*, p.179.
38 Gamba, *The Falklands/Malvinas*, p.179.
39 Gamba, *The Falklands/Malvinas*, p.104.
40 Gamba, *The Falklands/Malvinas*, p.110.
41 Gamba, *The Falklands/Malvinas*, p.110.
42 Gamba, *The Falklands/Malvinas*, p.110.
43 Gamba, *The Falklands/Malvinas*, p.110.
44 Gamba, *The Falklands/Malvinas*, p.110.
45 Gamba, *The Falklands/Malvinas*, p.110.
46 Gamba, *The Falklands/Malvinas*, p.110.

Chapter 3

1 Churchill, *The World Crisis*, p.599.
2 Cable, *Britain´s Naval*, p.37.
3 Rear Adm Allara, 'Statement at Comisión de Análisis', p.446.
4 Corbett, *Some Principles*, p.213.
5 Corbett, *Some Principles*, p.213.
6 Adm USN Train, 'Malvinas, un caso', p.238.
7 Finlan, *The Royal Navy*, p.66.
8 Vice Adm Lombardo (retd), *Malvinas*, p.86.
9 Vice Adm Lombardo (retd), *Malvinas*, p.86.
10 Finlan, *The Royal Navy*, p.66.
11 Russell, 'How Exocet', pp.38-47.
12 Hart Dyke, *Four Weeks in May*, p.92.
13 Hart Dyke, *Four Weeks in May*, p.80.
14 Adm Woodward et al, *One Hundred Days*, pp.272-273.
15 Till, *Maritime Strategy*, p.270.
16 Rattembach, *Informe*, ¶ 808 sub-§c, p.219.
17 Rear Adm Büsser, interview, 26 Mar 1991, p.70.
18 Büsser, *Operación*, pp.121-144.
19 Vice Adm Lombardo, *Informe Oficial*, p.34.
20 This section is based on the author's personal interviews with naval officers who participated in the operation.
21 Lt Luna led one of the Marine squads who took part in the action.
22 Capt Figueroa (retd), 'Malvinas: las fallas', pp.117-133.
23 Vice Adm Alfonso (retd), 'La corbeta Guerrico', pp.49-52.
24 Rattenbach, *Informe*, p.628.
25 Brig Maj Menéndez (retd), *Malvinas: testimonio*, p.101.
26 Finlan, *The Royal Navy*, p.93.
27 Till, *Seapower*, p.173.
28 Fuchida et al., *Midway*, p.247.
29 Vice Adm Lombardo, *Malvinas*, p.88.
30 Thatcher, *The Downing Street Years*, p.228.
31 Middlebrook, *The Fight for the Malvinas*, pp.217-218.
32 Rattenbach, *Informe*, p.227.
33 As told by Capt Alejandro Tierno to this author.
34 Vice Adm Lombardo, *Informe Oficial*, p.79.
35 Vice Adm Lombardo, *Informe Oficial*, pp.79-81.
36 Capt Coli (retd), 'La Flota de Mar', pp.87-108.
37 Vice Adm Lombardo, *Informe Oficial*, p.121.
38 Sciaroni, 'Satélites', pp.119-134.
39 Ward, *Sea Harrier*, p.124.
40 Ward, *Sea Harrier*, p.124.
41 Middlebrook, *The Fight for the Malvinas*, p.103.
42 Adm Woodward et al., *One Hundred Days*, p.167.
43 Based on interviews with Capt (retd) Washington Barcena and Capt (retd) Horacio Grassi, former Cdrs of destroyer Belgrano's escorts.
44 Based on aforementioned interviews. See also: Mayorga, *No Vencidos*, p.261 and Bonzo, H. *1093 Tripulantes del Crucero ARA General Belgrano* (Buenos Aires: Instituto de Publicaciones Navales, 2004).
45 The author spent a year during 1980 at the Naval Academy with the three of them: midshipman Emilio Carlos Torlaschi, Juan José Aguirre and Gerardo Esteban Sevilla. The first of them was in command of the author's Brigade during the initial training.
46 Adm Lombardo, in D. Cavallieri, *Hasta la última*, p.101.
47 Vice Adm Lombardo, *Malvinas*, p.123.
48 Adm Anaya in *Gente*, p.90.
49 Hughes, *Fleet Tactics*, p.5.
50 Capt Jorge Colombo, CO of the 2nd Naval Air Squadron which sank HMS *Sheffield*.
51 Capt Colombo, cited in E. Castrillon et al., 'Nostalgias', p.3.
52 Vice Adm Rótolo (retd), interview, 13 June 2013.
53 Lt Cdr Robles, interview, 5 Dec 1979.
54 Figueroa, 'La vida a bordo', pp.60–67.
55 Adm Woodward et al., *One Hundred Days*, pp.259-261.
56 Vice Adm Rótolo (retd), in Sicalesi et al., 'El hundimiento', pp.63-64.
57 Vice Adm Rótolo (retd), in Sicalesi et al., 'El hundimiento', pp.63-64.
58 Svendsen, 'Acciones', pp.39-49. See also Bóveda, 'Helicópteros', pp.66-76.
59 Sylvester, interview, p.20.
60 See: Castro Fox, Rodolfo, *Yo fui piloto aviador naval* (Buenos Aires: Ed. Jorge F. Nuñez Padin, 2002).
61 Castrillón et al., 'Nostalgias', pp.3-4.
62 Inskip, *Ordeal by Exocet*, pp.74-75.
63 Capt Colombo (retd), in Castrillón et al., p.2
64 Bóveda, 'Operación', p.82.
65 Maisonneuve et al., *La Guerre des Malouines*, translated manuscript (unpaginated).
66 Maisonneuve et al., *La Guerre des Malouines*, translated manuscript (unpaginated).
67 Craig, *Call for Fire*, p.69.
68 Jenkins, interview, 8 Apr 2007.
69 Bóveda, 'Operación', p.82.
70 Mayorga, *No Vencidos*, p.436.
71 Carballo, *Dios y los*, p.11.
72 Adm Mozzarelli (retd), 'Nuestra Fuerza', p.38.
73 See: Bóveda, Jorge R., *Malvinas: la odisea del Submarino Santa Fe* (Buenos Aires: Instituto de Publicaciones Navales, 2007).
74 Bóveda, 'ARA Salta', pp.13-15.
75 Bóveda, 'Uno', pp.113-126. See also Sheina, 'Where were those', pp.115-120.
76 Middlebrook, *The Fight for the Malvinas*, p.217.
77 Adm Robacio (retd), 'El Batallón', p.145.
78 Middlebrook, *The Fight for the Malvinas*, p.218.
79 Middlebrook, *The Fight for the Malvinas*, p.218.

80 Hastings et al., *The Battle for the Falklands*, p.303.
81 Adm Robacio (retd), 'El Batallón', p.153.
82 Middlebrook, *The Fight for the Malvinas*, p.218.
83 The author had the privilege of being a close friend of Rear Adm Pérez´s family throughout his life, as he was a very close friend of the author's father and a fellow graduate of the same class (1958) at the Naval Academy.
84 Rear Adm Pérez (retd), 'Operación Uka', pp.211-217.
85 Inskip, *Ordeal by Exocet*, pp.163-164.
86 Rear Adm Pérez (retd), 'Operación', p.217.
87 Thatcher, *The Downing Street Years*, p.228.

Chapter 4

1 Malvinas: gesta e incompetencia by Lt. Gral (Retired) M. Balza, Planeta, 2008, pp.287
2 Decree 1714/2009.
3 Horacio, *La Casa Está en Orden*, p.312.
4 Diamint, *Sin Gloria*, p.460.
5 Weinberger, *Fighting for Peace*, pp.429-430.
6 Ministerio de Defensa, *Libro Blanco*, p.98.
7 Rosenthal, 'La Armada Argentina', pp.255-268.

ABOUT THE AUTHOR

Jorge Rafael Bóveda was born in Buenos Aires and educated in England and Argentina. He graduated as a lawyer from the University of Buenos Aires and currently works as a specialist in Labor Law. In addition, he holds a Master's Degree in Strategic Studies from the National Defense University in Buenos Aires. He is a permanent member of the Editorial Board of the Argentine Naval War College Review. He has written many articles on Argentine naval history published in Argentina, the United Kingdom and Spain, and is the author of the first book on Argentine submarine operations during the Falklands/Malvinas War of 1982. He was twice awarded the best history paper by the Argentine Naval Centre and is a member of the Argentine Institute of Military History. Mr Bóveda lives in Buenos Aires, Argentina.